Surfer's Code

Surfer's Code

12 Simple Lessons

for Riding Through Life

Shaun Tomson
with Patrick Moser

Gibbs Smith, Publisher
Salt Lake City

First Edition
09 08 07 06   5 4 3 2

Text © 2006 Shaun Tomson with Patrick Moser
Photo credits on page 192

Published by
Gibbs Smith, Publisher
P.O. Box 667
Layton, Utah 84041

Orders: 1.800.748.5439
www.gibbs-smith.com

Designed by Steve Rachwal
Printed and bound in Hong Kong

ISBN 1-4236-0076-2
Library of Congress Control Number: 2006925305

Contents

Introduction

I had not been back to South Africa for eight years. I had left the country in 1995, right at the end of the Apartheid era. Although I had grown up in the resort town of Durban, I had spent much of the 1970s and '80s traveling the globe as a professional surfer. Now, in 2003, I had been invited back to Durban to celebrate the twenty-fifth anniversary of my six-year winning streak, from 1973 to 1978, in South Africa's oldest and most prestigious professional surf contest, the Gunston 500.

On my first day at the beach *I saw a sight that I could never have imagined* while growing up. I was hurrying down the sand to take part in a surfing exhibition when I looked up and saw, coming directly toward me, three very attractive young women walking with a man. The first was a lovely Hindu girl—I could tell by the bindi (the red dot) on her forehead. She had long dark hair, wore a tiny bikini, and her belly button was pierced. She had one arm thrown around a black girl on her left side, and the other draped around the neck of an Indian guy on her right. Directly behind them walked a young woman in a full Muslim chador.

I was so surprised that I nearly dropped my surfboard.

It was amazing for me to see these different ethnic groups on the beach together for a surf contest. Everyone was getting along as if it were the most natural thing in the world. I was accustomed to such sights from my travels around the world, but never in South Africa. The country had changed so quickly. *Through the power and faith of one man, Nelson Mandela, the whole society changed.* People often talk about change happening incrementally. Certainly the rights of the nonwhite population — especially the blacks — came about through decades of struggle. But when Mandela came to power, our whole society—our entire lives—changed within a matter of weeks. And it happened peacefully.

I had been part of the privileged white society. The city of Durban sits along South Africa's eastern flank, one thousand miles north of the Cape of Good Hope. Durban is South Africa's busiest port city, home to over three million people, and also the country's most popular resort town. Located on the shores of the Indian Ocean, Durban has a pleasant climate and some of the best beach-break waves in the world.

Durban was a segregated city when I was growing up. The blacks (mostly Zulu) lived in a section of town known as Kwamashu. Whites — most of us from English rather than Dutch descent — lived in our section of town which we simply called Durban. The Indians remained close to their commercial district, an area known as Grey Street. *Blacks, whites, Indians, we all attended our own schools.* If men and women of different color had business to complete in the same building downtown, the blacks walked in one door, and the whites walked in another. A white business owner might have black employees, but other than such arrangements there was little interaction among the three different societies. Such a severe division among the people of South Africa was the strongest weapon used by the government to remain in

« Many people do not know that Gandhi lived in Durban for almost twenty years. This is the city where he developed and practiced his philosophy of Satyagraha, which included nonviolent resistance. »

power. When the legendary Hawaiian surfer Eddie Aikau came to Durban in 1972 to surf in the Gunston 500, he was refused lodging at the local whites-only hotel. Eddie ended up in a hotel with my family and had to be issued a special permit to surf at the beach. These were the daily realities of living and surfing in Durban during Apartheid.

By 2003 those divisions had completely broken down. I even had the chance on that same trip to visit Mahatma Gandhi's memorial. Many people do not know that Gandhi lived in Durban for almost twenty years. This is the city where he developed and practiced his philosophy of *Satyagraha,* which included nonviolent resistance. Gandhi had lived in an area where whites did not venture while I was growing up. I had always heard stories that if a white person ever went to that section of town, he could get himself killed. Much of the area was burned down during the race riots of 1987.

After the riots the Indian government paid to rebuild Gandhi's house, and it was amazing for me not only to go down there, but to see Gandhi's original writings on display. Not only had he developed much of his philosophy right there in the city where I had grown up, but his influence had extended so far from Durban: to India's prime minister Indira Gandhi, to Martin Luther King Jr., to President John F. Kennedy, then eventually back to South Africa and Nelson Mandela in his struggle against Apartheid. *I have always been amazed how a few simple ideas from one man could have such a strong influence on South Africa and the entire world.*

I am very proud to be a surfer. In South Africa we were always considered professional athletes, luckily avoiding the stereotypes that surround surfers here in the United States. But since this is my home now, and my son, Mathew, is an American, I hope to change that image in positive ways. I did not invent the lessons in this book. The ideas were already out there, part of the daily rituals of a large and diverse surf community. My idea was simply to pull them together. *Surfer's Code* is not a system of rules that tells you what you must and must not do. I rate these twelve lessons as a personal commitment that I have made as a surfer, that some of my friends have made, to reaffirm our commitment to the ocean and to one another. It would make me very happy to know that someone had passed this wisdom along to another surfer out there, especially a younger one who is just learning to surf or who wants to learn. I have given copies of the lessons to the top surfers in the world, and they are always stoked to have them. Younger surfers get stoked about them too because they understand the many layers of meaning within each one.

It has been my experience that younger surfers need guidance. What is more, they *want* guidance. They *want* instruction. What they do not want is be left out there in the lineup to fend for themselves. I first began *Surfer's Code* as a means of steering younger surfers in the right direction: giving them practical insights into what surfers do, and how they act, in the surf zone. I soon learned that each of the lessons for life in the water also had meaning for life on land. And not just for younger surfers, for all of us. In a sport growing more crowded every day, with so many different people now entering the water, a few simple ideas can go a long way to help bring everyone together.

I was never the best student in ancient languages at my school, but there is one word that I have had cause to remember over the years: *Code*. It comes from the Latin *codex*, a tablet of wood covered with wax that people used to write on. You can see why, as a surfer, I might remember that one. Code came to mean more than the piece of

« In a sport growing more crowded every day, with so many different people now entering the water, a few simple ideas can go a long way to help bring everyone together. »

wood itself: it stood for the system of principles written into the wax. *Surfer's Code* is a handful of principles that I have gathered over a lifetime of surfing, compiled from the marks left by my own waxed-up tablets on waves around the world.

I have competed for many years at the highest level, and I have won professional events and honors at the most famous beaches around the world. But if a young surfer can read *Surfer's Code,* learn some useful information, and ultimately get more enjoyment in and out of the ocean because of this book, then it will be the best thing I have ever done in my surfing career.

Stay stoked,

Shaun Tomson

SANTA BARBARA, CALIFORNIA

1

I Will Never Turn My Back

on the Ocean

Above: My father, Ernest "Chony" Tomson, two weeks before he died from a heart attack in Durban, South Africa (1923–1981).

Right: Racing through the tube at Off The Wall in Hawai'i, 1978 (photo: Dan Merkel).

Zambezi sharks are one of the world's most dangerous predators. Essentially saltwater creatures, they have been known to swim more than 600 miles up river in search of prey. They thrive in shallow, murky waters and are particularly prevalent in my hometown of Durban, South Africa, where they account for a very high percentage of attacks and fatalities. These days large nets strung out three hundred yards from shore protect the beachgoers in Durban. *But back in 1957, during a month now referred to as "Dark December," seven swimmers were attacked by Zambezi sharks, and five of them died.*

My father, Chony Tomson, was one of South Africa's most promising swimmer. In 1947, at the age of 24, he was training to represent South Africa in the Empire and in the Olympic Games. He loved to compete and took an enormous amount of pride in winning, but he was always able to place winning into a larger perspective. He felt that with all the problems in the world at the time—he had volunteered as a tail gunner in the South African Air Force during World War II—that sports competition was one area people could get on together and interact with one another in an honorable way. Sports were dear to him—a way of building character—and, win or lose, he prized good sportsmanship above all else.

He did not make it to the Olympic trials that year or any other. Back home in Durban we had a long stretch of beach bounded on the southern side by a big headland called the Bluff. The Durban city beaches then headed north from the Bluff, divided up by jetties that produced tremendous surf. One day while he was out swimming at a place called South Beach, just having fun riding waves on a little wooden board that we called a dumper board, a Zambezi shark attacked him. It hit him so hard that his entire body was lifted out of the water. When he dropped back down he was missing most of his right biceps.

He later told me that he had never seen the ocean clear so fast. Men scrambled up the pilings of the pier, shredding their hands and chests on the sharp mussel shells. In all the confusion and all the blood, people on the beach at first thought there had been multiple attacks. One swimmer managed to keep his head in the chaos, and he pulled my father to shore. They rushed him to Addington Hospital on the beachfront, and the doctors immediately packed his arm in ice. Luckily it was high summer and all the beach hotels had laid in their store of ice for the tourists. My father's rescue actually became local legend and for many years afterward, when I had gained fame as a surfer, men would come up to me and ask, «AREN'T YOU CHONY'S SON? I HELPED PULL YOUR FATHER IN.» I am sure they were well-meaning, but if I counted all the people who had told me that story over the years, the list of rescuers would swell to the length of a set wave at Jeffrey's Bay (one of the longest point breaks in the world, by the way).

He never regained the use of his right arm, and he did not like to talk about the attack. If one of us kids—my younger brother Paul or my sister Tracy—ever asked him about it, he would always reply with a joke. «THE SHARK DIED OF BLOOD POISONING,» he'd tell us with a laugh. Or, «I DON'T KNOW WHO GOT THE BIGGER SHOCK, ME OR THE SHARK.» My mother later told me that he experienced terrible nightmares. ***But because of his sense of humor, we thought him totally unself-conscious of the terrible scars that the shark teeth's had left on his body.*** I never considered him disabled in any way, but his arm steadily withered from lack of use, and his right fist remained in a permanent clench.

Immediately after the attack he traveled to San Francisco for extensive surgery on his right arm, a process that also included a series of very painful skin grafts from his stomach. As a child I remembered asking him about those scars. My father simply smiled and said, «ACK-ACK,» like anti-aircraft fire, a reference to his stint as a tail gunner during the war. Sometimes when I think about his answer, I recall his great sense of humor. Other times I imagine a wound so deep and so traumatic that a man reaches for the horrors of war rather than stir up memories of an even more painful time in his life.

After leaving San Francisco he recuperated for several months in the Hawaiian Islands. Here was a man with a tremendous swimming career ahead of him, now unable to do what he most loved and reminded of that fact every time he looked down at an arm he could not move and a hand he could not open. He had every right to be bitter about the experience and to *turn his back on the ocean.*

Yet some of my earliest memories are of my father taking me by the hand and leading me down into the water at North Beach. He never gave up on his love for the ocean, and he instilled that love in me from a very young age.

We used to call going for a swim, going for a *Tiger*. We spoke in a rhyming slang in the area of Durban where I grew up, inherited from the Cockneys in England who had emigrated to South Africa and brought their particular way of speaking with them. So we didn't say money, we said *Tom Funny*. Sharks were called *Johnnys* or *Johnny Darks* (and so the reference to "Dark December"). When someone disappeared in the ocean we'd say, «A JOHNNY TOOK 'EM,» or, «THEY GOT HIT BY A JOHNNY.» So a swim was called a *Tiger Tim*. I'd say to my father, «C'MON, LET'S GO FOR A TIGER, LET'S GO FOR A TIGER.» I was six or seven years old. I remember him holding my hand and walking me down to the water.

In South Africa during the summertime heavy rains caused the Umgeni River to swell, and red silt washed down to the ocean and clouded the water, making it very hard to see beneath the surface. Also in the summertime a northeasterly wind blew down from the

« Imagine a man profoundly aware of the dangers of the ocean—himself savaged by a shark that destroyed his swimming career—and yet here he was placing his first-born son, whom he loved deeply, straight out there in the ocean and being enthusiastic about it . . . »

Mozambique Channel, and big jellyfish floated in with their long, painful stingers. And of course there were always the Johnnys lurking about.

Imagine a man profoundly aware of the dangers of the ocean — himself savaged by a shark that destroyed his swimming career — and yet here he was placing his first-born son, whom he loved deeply, straight out there in the ocean and being enthusiastic about it — teaching me how to swim, teaching me how to bodysurf, and loving the fact that I enjoyed a career where I spent most every day in the ocean. And his enthusiasm radiated out to the whole surfing community, especially in Durban. He sponsored a great number of young guys to encourage them to keep surfing, and he watched us all the time with binoculars to see who was surfing well and to offer advice. And he did it all in a very special way so that we wanted to do well both for him and for our own sakes. He was never overbearing about it. He understood that competition was obviously very important, but he made us keep the idea of winning in perspective because he wanted us to have a great time doing it.

So my earliest lesson about the ocean I learned from my father. I heard many years afterward that the Hawaiian beachboys at Waikiki have a similar saying. When they placed a bronze statue of the great swimmer and surfer, Duke Kahanamoku, at Waikiki in 1990, they faced him out toward Kalakaua Avenue so that tourists would have a good photo opportunity, with the beautiful beach of Kuhio in the background. The local beachboys just laughed and shook their heads. «DUKE NEVER WOULDA TURNED HIS BACK ON THE OCEAN,» they said. Obviously, from a practical point of view, the lesson is particularly important in Hawai'i since there is no continental shelf to slow

The wave closest to Hawaiian style power was Cave Rock, a hard breaking tube only 20 minutes from my home in Durban, South Africa. In July 1976, there were no shark nets, so my father was always on the lookout (photo: Dan Merkel).

swells down, and waves can break suddenly and with a tremendous amount of force. Those who turn their back on the ocean risk an abrupt and painful introduction to the coral reef. For the Waikiki beachboys, turning your back on the ocean is not only foolish, but it also shows disrespect for the ocean's power. My father most probably picked up the saying from the beachboys while he was recuperating in Hawai'i. Most his life he was a beachboy himself.

WILL NEVER TURN MY BACK ON THE OCEAN

A friend from America asked me one time, «WHY DID IT WORK IN SOUTH AFRICA? WHY WAS THERE SUCH A PEACEFUL CHANGE-OVER TO DEMOCRACY?» I told her it was because of Nelson Mandela. After twenty-seven years in prison, he left without bitterness, and with a spirit of reconciliation. I grew up with a father who also carried no bitterness about an experience that destroyed something he loved. *It is a very rare person, at whatever level of society, who does not look over his shoulder and dwell on the past* and who can move forward in a positive way for himself and for others.

My family stayed out of politics. I can clearly remember my father's warning before I left for University in 1974: «SHAUN, DON'T GET INVOLVED IN POLITICS. I DO NOT WANT YOU LOCKED UP.» Just as he understood the unseen dangers in the ocean, he knew similar dangers existed during Apartheid. Getting thrown in jail was a very real possibility for speaking out in South Africa. We rarely heard about Nelson Mandela while I was growing up, for instance, because few in the government ever spoke of him. A Johnny took 'em, so to speak, and while his plight made news outside the country, within the South Africa where I grew up he remained this very shadowy fig-ure who had been thrown in prison for what at the time was per-ceived as terrorism. It is difficult to express the jolt to your psyche when you have fundamental beliefs completely upended. I grew up believing Mandela an enemy of the state. Then later I found out that everything I knew about him—his goals, his actions, his ideals—had all been created by propaganda in the South African government. *I realized that I had no genuine knowledge of the*

man or his mission for South Africa at all. It was a very disorienting experience, another casualty of a political system that relies upon separating citizens from one another.

My father and I had a special relationship and a very rare relationship. I followed his advice at University and afterward. Once I became world surfing champion in 1977 and gained a lot of recognition in South Africa, I could have used that recognition to push for political change. But I never did. I was reluctant to go against my father, my family, my friends—all the people who has supported my career for so long. *They were the South Africa I was so proud of and wanted to represent,* not a political policy or party that I personally abhorred.

I had conflicting feelings about the whole situation. These actually did not surface publicly until 1985 when I made a speech at the annual end-of-the-year awards ceremony. The world tour had wrapped up that year at Bells Beach, in Victoria, Australia, and the ceremony was held in the nearby town of Torquay. It was a big bash for the Australians since their native son, Tom Carroll, had won the title. I had come in a close second. In fact I had been leading the ratings going into the final Australian leg of the tour and ended up losing by a slim margin. Not only did Tom win the world championship for the second year in a row, but he did it while being sponsored by my apparel company, Instinct, which I had begun several years prior. Before the awards ceremony Tom suddenly announced that he would be boycotting all surf competition in South Africa in the upcoming year.

I was stunned and deeply hurt. I found out about the announcement secondhand rather that directly from Tom. We had sponsored him before he had won his first pro contest, and he had won two world titles riding for Instinct. I stood at the podium and accepted my award for runner-up, knowing that Tom would be speaking right after me. I had all these emotions and thoughts running through my head. I had just lost the world championship in the last contest of the season, so on a personal level I was devastated. *It was the hardest loss of my career.* On a professional level I was equally devastated: Tom dropped us as a sponsor, so we had just lost our number one rider, a two-time world champion. It was a big blow for the entire company.

And what would happen to the world tour in the upcoming year? I had been there at its founding in 1976 and had spent the intervening years working to build and strengthen what is now known as the Association of Surfing Professionals, the ruling body of the world tour. It was a fragile organization back then: a country or company might sponsor an event one year, and then drop out the next. Every year we scrambled for an umbrella sponsor to support the administrative aspects of running a world tour and so ensure that the athletes would make enough money to travel and compete. South Africa had been a mainstay of the tour since the very beginning, hosting a contest called the Gunston 500, which I had won six times. Boycotting events in South Africa would be a slap to a sponsor that had been a longtime supporter of the tour, and also to the memory of my father (he had passed away in 1981), who had helped found the event.

I had all these things to deal with as I looked out at a crowd of surfers whom I traveled with, competed against, gotten along with, even sponsored in the case of Tom Carroll, and I didn't know what to say. The normal contingent of reporters and news cameras

« I had learned from my father that sports could bring people together, that a forum like the Olympics could and should rise above the politics of individual nations. I strongly believe that today. »

had doubled in size since Tom's notoriety as the world champ. His announcement of the boycott had attracted the attention of the Prime Minister of Australia, Robert Hawke, who rallied around his decision. For my part there was no question of political retaliation from South Africa, since I had become an American citizen the year before, in 1984. But *boycotting events in South Africa ran against everything I believed sports competition to be: a way to bring people together, not separate them.* The South African government had used Apartheid (meaning "apartness" in Afrikaans) as an instrument of cruelty to separate people, not only whites from blacks (and Indians and Coloureds), but black ethnic groups and social classes from one another. Surfers were employing the tactics of the enemy and using the sport of surfing as a political weapon.

I told the surfers and the media that night I thought they were all bowing to political pressure. The world tour needed them in South Africa, and South Africa needed them. My former country had become geographically and socially isolated in the world. This was a country, I reminded them, that had not even gotten television until 1976 — one hour in English, one hour in Afrikaans — and even then it was used to reinforce government control and isolationist policies. I did not think that further isolation was the answer.

I had learned from my father that sports could bring people together, that a forum like the Olympics could and should rise above the politics of individual nations. I strongly believe that today. And yet I know that Tom Carroll took his position based on his own strong beliefs and a desire to help remedy a great injustice and the cruelty of Apartheid.

I still miss my father every day. I used to phone him after every event, often telling him that I had not done so well, then busting him up with the news that I had won. It was a joke we liked to share and one that had I learned from him. I will never forget the first time he pulled it on me in the Gunston 500. He acted as a spotter during the contest. He would stand in the judges' tower and call off the colors of the jerseys as the surfers stood up to assist the judges in their scoring. In 1973 I was standing on the presentation stage with five other finalists. I could see my father sitting up in the judges' tower about twenty yards away, and I knew he could see the scores. It had been a very close final. At one point I looked up at him for some form of assurance. I remember him slowly shaking his head at me, subtly giving me the thumbs down. I was devastated. When the results were announced minutes later, I had won! He had known all along, of course, but he could not let a great opportunity for a joke slip by. It was my first victory in a professional contest, one of many that we enjoyed together.

I remember the phone call I got from my mother while competing in Australia in 1981. She told me simply that he was gone. No warning, no time for me to prepare, just my mother on the other end saying how terribly sorry she was. I think she had never stopped loving him even though they had divorced many years before. A son measures his own mortality by his parents. I was young, strong, and invincible and had never even contemplated death. After the previous event — where I had placed fifth — I had not phoned my father as I normally did. I had not wanted to talk about my poor performance. I did not even have the chance to say good-bye.

Each person has a different take on what it means never to turn your back on the ocean. When I speak to groups of kids about it today, they immediately get the multiple meanings, and they tell me right off that it is about the environment and giving something back to the ocean. *The ocean is alive, they say, and it helps keep us alive so we should not just take pleasure from it and walk away.* They are so much more aware of the environment than my generation, and they understand, on an intuitive level, that any relationship where one half always takes from the other is unhealthy.

For me, I'll always think about my father and the love and respect he had for the ocean. If he could find a way to enjoy the ocean and make it a part of his life after what happened to him, certainly the rest of us can too.

2

I Will Paddle Around the Impact Zone

Turning around the impact zone at the Banzai Pipeline in December 1975 (photo: Steve Wilkings).

« This zone where waves give up their energy and where systematic water motions give way to violent turbulence is the surf. It is the most exciting part of the ocean. »

WILLIARD BASCOM

Willard Bascom's book *Waves and Beaches* has many interesting things to say about how and why waves work. Though quite technical on occasion (Bascom was an oceanographer), I recommend the book to anyone who really wants to understand the ocean. The zone Bascom refers to above is what surfers call *the Impact Zone,* and Bascom is absolutely right. It is the most exciting part of the ocean and by far the most dangerous. Water crashes into land and creates waves while surfers paddle around each other competing for those waves. The surfers who are not careful get caught in the middle of all that chaos, and they can either get themselves hurt or cause someone else to get hurt.

It doesn't have to be that way. This lesson is basic to anyone who can keep their eyes open and extend a little courtesy to other surfers in the water. In a larger sense, this lesson reminds us how *the ocean teaches us the right time to exercise patience and when to seize opportunity.*

When surfers arrive at the beach, they stop and look out at the waves. What are they looking at? They are reading the ocean as one might read a book. They look at the waves and gauge their size, their frequency, where they break, and in what direction they are breaking. (Do they peel to the right? To the left? Fold over all at once?) They read wind and swell direction. (Are waves coming from the northwest? The west? The southwest? Or a combination of these directions?) They are also locating any riptides that might help them get out to where the waves are breaking. They check the tide and whether it is coming in or going out. Surfers consider all of these signs simultaneously or nearly so, spinning various combinations in their minds. All the signs bear upon how the waves are breaking that day and whether a surfer will paddle out, wait a little longer, or go home and climb back into bed.

Always, of course, surfers are looking to see if there are other surfers out in the water floating around the impact zone. So most surfers *take time to look and to consider.* Those who take the time to consider are halfway there to being considerate. Let me explain what I mean.

If the waves are at all decent, surfers will get stoked, as they say, and they will want to get straight out there and have some fun. I'm all for it. The considerate ones will paddle around the impact zone. Those who do not know better, or who should know better, will take the shortest path to where the waves are breaking and paddle *through* the impact zone. This can be a very dangerous and irresponsible thing to do. They not only jeopardize their own safety, but the safety of any surfer who might be coming down the line on a wave. In order to save a minute or two of paddling, they take the chance of ruining a wave for someone else. Surfers reserve a special name for someone who does that: *a kook, and it is the worst insult one surfer can throw at another.* Being a kook is not about the clothes you wear, the board you ride, or even how long you have been surfing. It's about how you act in the water. You can get as radical as you want in the surf and still be considerate of others.

My most favorite place to surf these days is Rincon, near Santa Barbara, California. Santa Barbara sits along the coast a hundred miles north of Los Angeles. Back in the 1950s and '60s, when most of the surf population was centered either in the L.A. area or south of there, surfers would make the trek up Highway 1 during the fall and wintertime, when Rincon breaks best. As you drive along the coast, you can actually see the swells breaking from the road. Before the county built parking lots near Rincon Point, surfers would simply park along the shoulder and walk down the cobblestone rocks to the ocean.

Rincon became known as the *Queen of the Coast,* arguably the best single wave in the entire state of California. Its long and beautiful waves give surfers fast, exciting rides. I love to carve on long walls of water, and it is my personal bias that riding these kind of waves is the true measure of a good surfer (mostly because I grew up riding similar waves at the Bay of Plenty in South Africa). Because of its beautiful and exciting waves, Rincon is also one of the most crowded surf spots in the world. On any given swell you might see *hundreds of surfers in the water,* and a good number of them are likely to be young, inexperienced, or simply inconsiderate.

« When a good swell storms out of the west or northwest and wraps around Rincon Point, the Queen of the Coast is really one of the most beautiful sights you will ever see. »

The wave at Rincon starts breaking way out on a point of land and rumbles all the way down alongside the cobblestone beach that skirts Highway 1. The break is divided up into three main sections: Farthest out is *Indicator,* followed by the *Rivermouth* (directly in front of Rincon Creek), and finally the *Cove,* the most popular and crowded part of the break. On rare occasions a surfer can link all three sections for an incredible ride the length of five football fields. When you consider that the average ride at most beach breaks is only a few seconds, you begin to understand why surfers love Rincon. When a good swell storms out of the west or northwest and wraps around Rincon Point, the Queen of the Coast is really one of the most beautiful sights you will ever see.

But rather than start at the top of the beach and paddle around the breaking wave, a good number of surfers will paddle directly out through the impact zone—straight into the face of the wave rather than around and behind it. They might save a hundred yards of pad- dling, perhaps a minute or two, but it is inconsiderate because a shortcut for them might mean a spoiled wave for somebody else. Because of the severe crowding at Rincon, it is vitally important to be careful when paddling out. It is just too dangerous to paddle through the break, and yet countless people do it. I see the most ter- rible collisions, injuries, frayed tempers, and even fights, all because someone wanted to take *a shortcut.* If you consider the most talented and successful performers in any field, none of them ever made it to the top by relying on shortcuts.

There's a lesson for all of us.

I love taking the longer way around. It is not only safer and allows me to keep my hair dry on those cold winter mornings when Rincon breaks best, but I can loosen up as I paddle and watch the other surfers fly down those long walls of water. Surfing has always been an exciting spectator sport and not only from the beach. I enjoy watching the other surfers perform; it gives me ideas for my own surfing and allows me to see where the lineup is and to be mindful of any critical sections in the wave. Best of all, I do not have to worry about starting my session by getting run over by a surfboard.

When I surf Rincon and see young boys and girls paddling straight out, I always paddle up to them. I tell them, «LISTEN, YOU SEE THAT SURFER COMING DOWN THE LINE? HE'S GOING TO RUN YOU OVER. FOLLOW ME.» Then I take them around the break. As a father I think it is important the way we communicate these practices to our kids. *We all have a responsibility to pass on our knowledge.* You might have your own code, and it does not have to be these particular lessons. But it is important to share that wisdom because no one else is going to do it. People do not tell kids, except their own children, how to act in the surf and the kinds of things to avoid. I mentioned this in the introduction of this book and it bears repeating: *kids need guidance, they want guidance,* and you will make their experience and everybody's experience in the water a whole lot better if you take the time to help them out and point them in the right direction.

I learned this lesson surfing the Bay of Plenty. I mentioned the jetties stretching along the coast where I grew up that produce fantastic surf. A dozen of us used to surf the place on a consistent basis back in the late 1960s and early '70s. We were all good surfers

Skip Frye, November 1964, paddling out into a set of perfect waves at Cojo, Bixby Ranch, California (photo: Ron Stoner).

and respectful of one another. We developed a code among ourselves that we would wait our turn when waves came. The person who had been waiting the longest was entitled to the next wave, and if you tried to paddle around that person to get into a better position, someone would always say something to you. It kept an amazing sense of order out in the water, and one of the results was that we paddled around the impact zone so that we did not ruin anyone else's ride.

At many places in the world, if there are two of you out and a wave pops up, that other surfer is going to paddle around you to get on the inside and grab the wave. Surfers have an unspoken rule that *the surfer closest to the peak (where the wave breaks first) has the right of way.* Getting to that spot before the other guy creates a lot of competition in the lineup, and sometimes conflict. Since the early '90s there have been a lot more surfers riding longboards, and this has proven to be a boon for many people who find these craft easier to learn on. The new longboards are lighter than ever before, and anyone with a reasonable sense of balance can learn to stand up and ride a wave very quickly. But many people choose to ride longboards for the wrong reasons. Not because they love that artistic kind of surfing where they can ride the wave with style and grace, but simply because they want to catch more waves. And because they can get more waves on a longer board, they take more waves. I always say something to people when I think they are being greedy. I say, «WHY DON'T YOU JUST WAIT YOUR TURN? THERE ARE OTHER SURFERS OUT HERE.»

Perhaps I am out of line when I say something, but I really cannot help myself. *It often boils down to common courtesy in the water.* I know the system that I grew up with in South Africa probably would not work at places like Rincon, with hundreds of surfers in the water, but we can still adapt that same sense of courtesy and extend it to others even at the most crowded breaks and make it a better session for everyone.

We live in a society of instant gratification.
We all want to get where we are going really quickly, and we want results yesterday. I fall into this trap myself. I cannot tell you how many days I sit behind my desk and get so caught up in what my clothing reps are doing and how sales are going and when to start preparing for the next trade show that I often forget why I located my business in Santa Barbara in the first place: Because it's a beautiful little city, with quiet beaches and fantastic surf. Surfing has never been about getting results quickly. In fact, the reason why many people surf

is to get away from that mentality. *Surfing teaches patience.* On land, surfers cannot will a swell to appear. And though certain rituals have been passed down from Polynesian cultures to encourage the ocean to stir up swells, for all intents and purposes surfers cannot order up waves as they would a pizza. They have to wait for nature to make the call. *So surfers wait.* They keep their eyes on the horizon and they wait.

Surfing also teaches quality. I will

wager that it is not the number of waves that makes a session memorable for any given surfer, but that one beautiful wave that he or she waited for, picked off cleanly, and rode all the way into shore.

So take the time to paddle around the impact zone. You will get in the best shape of your life. And I have learned that *only when I am at my best — as a competitive surfer and a surfer in a competitive business — will I be able to take full advantage of the opportunities that come my way.*

[LESSON]

3

I Will Take the Drop
with Commitment

Banzai Pipeline 1982, on one of the most dangerous days I had ever seen. The swell jumped from 6 feet to 20 feet in 4 hours (photo: Jeff Divine).

In all the world, one surf spot always had an aura of danger surrounding it while I was growing up. It had the steepest, most formidable take-off. As a kid I remember watching movies that showed the most hor-rifying wipeouts there: surfers cartwheeling over the falls and getting driven into the coral reef, their boards broken, their bodies lacerated. Beyond being an extremely dangerous wave, it was also one of the most beautiful I had ever seen — the tropical blue water, the hypnotic cylinders only adding to its allure. It was the only place I had ever read about where a surfer had actually been killed.

The place is called *Pipeline* **on the North Shore of O'ahu.**

At most big-wave spots on the North Shore — Sunset Beach, Waimea Bay — the waves break rather far out to sea, so when you watch them from the beach they do not look as big as they really are; it is easy to get lulled into a false sense of confidence. Such waves have a slow-motion quality when they break, another optical illusion. Imagine the tempo of a whale leaping out of the ocean. This stunning beauty cloaks massive speed and force.

Pipeline does not provide such deceptions. It smashes into the reef fifty yards from the beach, practically at your feet. *You can actually feel the impact of these waves through the sand. It is frightening.* Yet for all of Pipeline's danger, the most difficult part is not taking that treacherous drop. This act is merely the culmination of a series of intense steps that

we all take when faced with a challenging situation, working—
sometimes agonizing—through fear and self-doubt as we build the
confidence to take that leap of faith in ourselves. ***The most
challenging part of riding Pipeline is commitment.***
And there are no guarantees of success, let alone survival.

I surfed Pipeline for the first time in 1970, when I was fifteen
years old. The wave had vaulted to center stage of the surf world
several years earlier with the widespread use of shorter surfboards.
Before the late '60s, Malibu had held that position: noseriding was
considered the ultimate maneuver at the time and Surfrider Beach—
with its long walls and modest-sized waves—the ultimate proving
ground. Shortboards changed all that. Along with the drop in length
and weight of boards came a new ideal among a younger generation
of surfers. We wanted to ride vertically on the wave, not horizontally;
we wanted to carve inside the wave rather than stand outside and
pose on the nose. Pipeline, with its vertical drop and cavernous walls,
became the perfect testing ground for our imaginations.

That first winter my father had taken me to Hawai'i as a Bar
Mitzva present, but we were there such a short time that I never saw
Pipeline break. The following year I stayed in a house right in front
of Pipeline, and my only real expectation was simply to paddle out
and take off on a wave. Imagine a young South African teenager trying to make his mark at one of the most dangerous and challenging
waves in the world. I had to walk down the beach in front of all the
Pipe houses—homes of famous surfers that had expansive front
porches where entire local crews watched and commented on every
session during the season. There has always been a tightly knit crew

at Pipeline, guys who dedicate their lives to riding the wave, and visiting surfers must pay their respects — and their dues — if they want to become accepted among the elite. So my first step to riding Pipeline took place on the beach, and it was internal. I was a nobody at the most dangerous break in the world, so I knew that I was likely to get hassled by the locals. I had to decide if I was going to work up the nerve to walk past those guys and paddle out.

In the end, I tucked my board under my arm and made that walk. Besides, I knew that the wave, and not the locals, meted out the real punishment. After paddling out to the lineup it took me half an hour to work up the courage to take off on a wave. The sets were not enormous — it was early in the season — but I was able to overcome the initial aura of Pipeline and the local crew simply by completing an act that I had completed a thousand times before. This is what I told myself: turn around, stroke into a wave, and ride it to shore. I doubt I impressed anyone that day. No matter. *My first task was not to convince the local crew that I belonged, but to convince myself.*

Still I remained intimidated, which was probably healthy. I surfed Pipeline several times over the next few winters, but honestly I never felt comfortable there. I did not truly work up the confidence to surf the place well — to learn how to take the drop with commitment — until I had spent a whole season on the North Shore in 1974.

Oddly enough, bricks were the turning point for me. A handful of bricks.

I had just finished my first year at university before arriving in Hawai'i for the winter season. I had won a big surf contest in South

Africa, the Gunston 500, so I had my stake. I had ordered a surfboard especially for the big Hawaiian waves from my shaper in South Africa, Spider Murphy. The year before I had stayed with Jeff Hakman, one of the top Hawaiian surfers of the era. Hakman had won all the prestigious events in the Islands—the Duke Kahanamoku Invitational at Sunset Beach (twice) and the Pipeline Masters. He had this beautiful big-wave gun made by a well-known shaper named Dick Brewer. At the time there was no better surfer and no better shaper to get a template from. So I took several pictures of the board from various angles and later gave them to Spider. I told him, «I WANT A BOARD EXACTLY LIKE THIS.» Any board good enough for Hakman was good enough for me.

Surfboards are basically sculptures in foam, with highly subtle changes in volume and line along the rails, around the deck and bottom, down through the tail. Therefore, it is impossible to make an exact replica of another board, especially from a set of photographs. Spider shaped the board for me, but it ended up not having as much curve along the bottom—what surfers call rocker—as Hakman's board. Without sufficient rocker, the nose of a surfboard will dig straight into the bottom of a wave on the drop, and the surfer will wipeout. *At a place like Pipeline, this can mean the difference between life and death.* I told Spider that Hakman's board had much more rocker toward the nose.

The best shapers are artists in their own right, but also improvisational craftsman who can be a bit temperamental when riders start making suggestions. Spider walked outside and grabbed a handful of bricks. He set my board down on a wooden rack and placed the bricks on the nose. Basically he just bent more rocker into the nose of the board.

What could I say? When he was done, the board looked like it had an awful lot of curve to it, now much more than Hakman's board. But Spider was my shaper, and I had already corrected him once. I picked up the board, ran my eyes over it like I was really admiring his work. «WELL,» I said, «THIS LOOKS GOOD.» I tucked it under my arm and left for the Islands.

It is hard to describe the excitement I felt flying into Honolulu, knowing that for the first time I would spend an entire season in the Islands. My friend picked me up at the airport, and we headed straight into the mountains toward the North Shore. It was November, the beginning of the winter storm season in the North Pacific. We drove through the mountain passes; just past the Dole pineapple fields the radio crackled a report of eight-to-ten-foot surf. We sped over the last ridge and saw a vista of blue water before us: Kaena Point to the south, on our left; Puena Point to the north, by the town of Haleiwa. We were up so high that I could see a break called Avalanche, six miles away, and gauge exactly how big the surf was by the white water rolling across the reef.

During this era the North Shore was the epicenter of the surf world in terms of performance. The best surfers in the world riding the latest designs in the most powerful waves congregated every year on a seven-mile stretch of reef and sand. Today the most radical surfing is taking place on the outer reefs by tow-in surfers, but in the 1970s, and for two decades afterward, the North Shore carried the torch. You were nobody in the surf world unless you had proven yourself on the North Shore. You had to show everyone that you could surf Waimea Bay just as well as Pipeline, Sunset Beach and Off The Wall just as well as Haleiwa or Laniakea. Most importantly at the time,

I had to prove to myself that I could surf all of these places with the best in the world.

My first session on the North Shore took place at Sunset Beach, perhaps the most technically challenging wave in the world with extremely dangerous currents, enormously shifting peaks. And once you have managed to line yourself up in the right position, there are the crowds and the tough local crew to deal with. I paddled my brand-new Spider Murphy board right into the middle of the pack. The swell was up, all the locals and traveling pros were there, and I wanted to make a big impression.

I did. The board was an absolute *dog*. I could not catch a single wave all afternoon. Lack of rocker makes the nose of a board knife into the water; but too much rocker does the opposite and pushes water. All those bricks Spider had put on my board had turned it into a big banana. Not only that, but *a big pink banana.* Instead of red—the classic big wave gun color—the tint job had gone wrong and the board came out pink.

Now I did have one other board with me. A company called Lightning Bolt had begun giving up-and-coming surfers free boards to help promote their name. Barry Kanaiaupuni, a fantastic surfer and well-known shaper on the North Shore, had made me a great board. Over the next couple of days Pipeline started to break, but I did not want to use the Lightning Bolt. If I broke it—and this was not uncommon at Pipeline—I would not have a board for the upcoming competitions. After my experience at Sunset Beach, there was no way I was going to use my Spider Murphy board in a contest. I could have asked Barry to build me another board, but honestly I would have been too embarrassed to tell him that I had broken the first one and needed another.

So the swell was up at Pipe, and I needed to practice. I had my Spider Murphy board. It was a real dog, but what choice did I have? I knew the board paddled slowly and pushed water; I understood there was a strong possibility it would hang me up in the worst possible place on the wave—right at the top in the lip—and that the wave would launch me head-first down into the coral. As I sat on the beach with my pink board considering all this—debating whether it might be better to wait for a smaller day, or until I had more experience on the board, or perhaps until the crowd thinned and the photographers had packed their gear—the heckling started. Voices from the Pipe houses rolled out the jokes.

"Hey," someone yelled. *"Where are you going with that pink banana?"*

One thing I knew: I could not afford any hesitation while I was in the water, or the wave was going to bury me in that reef. The holes in the coral are famous at Pipeline with razor-sharp cracks and ragged crevices that had trapped surfers' arms and legs, even their heads, after severe wipeouts. In an odd way, the voices gave me confidence. They brought me back to the first time I had surfed Pipeline and that walk down the beach. I decided to forget about my board. I blocked everything from my mind except trusting my instincts and the experience that had gotten me this far, and I made that walk again.

It is important to add that as deadly as Pipeline can be, it is even more intimidating for guys like me who surf it backside, with our left foot forward and our back to the wave. Instead of facing the wave as I pushed myself over that ledge — a much more stable position — I had to drop down while looking over my left shoulder. The best surfers at Pipeline during this time — Gerry Lopez, Rory Russell, Jackie Dunn — all rode facing the wave and so had a distinct advantage.

My wave finally came. I spun around and stroked hard into the face. I felt the sudden lift skyward and jumped immediately to my feet, pushing myself over the edge. Then something magical happened: the board slotted perfectly into the face. And I mean perfectly. I dropped down, cranked the turn around as hard and as fast as I could, and the board held tight because the bottom, with all that outrageous rocker, fit hand-in-glove with the equally outrageous angle of the breaking wave.

The rest of the ride really is history. I rode that board for the next five seasons at Pipeline and never wiped out on takeoff. Not once. I

« I decided to forget about my board. I blocked everything from my mind except trusting my instincts and the experience that had gotten me this far, and I made that walk again. »

won the Pipeline Masters the following year, the World Title two years later. Most importantly, I was able to do what every major design innovation in surfing has accomplished over the past century: open up new spaces on the wave. Suddenly I had equipment that would take me to places on the wave that I had previously only imagined, and this gave me a tremendous boost of confidence.

Since the late 1960s, when shortboards allowed surfers to ride inside the wave on a regular basis, tuberiding has remained the most challenging and the most thrilling part of surfing. Though boosting aerials — essentially surfing above the wave — has now become the prime focus for a younger generation, and tow-in surfing has taken the thrill of waveriding literally to new heights, for me tuberiding retains its prominence, and I think most surfers today would agree. *There is something very special about riding on a board while surrounded by moving water,* a rare phenomenon that takes guts and grace and skill to do successfully. I rode farther back in the tube than anyone else, with more control than anyone else, and with my new board I soon began actually *to carve* along the face of the wave while inside the tube. This allowed me to take much more control of the ride and to experience a part of the wave that had never previously been explored by any surfer — that is to say, a surfer who made it back out to tell the tale.

The impact of that day at Pipeline was both immediate and enduring. Maneuvers that are being performed inside waves today by the top surfers—Kelly Slater, Joel Parkinson, Andy and Bruce Irons— are all based on lines that I worked out in those first years on Spider Murphy's brick-nosed board. I was tremendously lucky because of the design fluke, but I was only able to take advantage of that luck after having worked through fears and doubts that could have kept me on the beach. I would never have gone on to win the Pipeline Masters, or to surf at the highest level of my life in those years from 1974 to 1978, if I had not worked up the nerve to walk down the beach at Pipeline when I was fifteen years old, if I had not ignored those voices from the Pipe houses and instead relied upon the voices within: *trust your instincts, trust your experience.* Just as being in the best shape has allowed me to take full advantage of opportunities in life, having confidence has put me in the position of benefiting the most from lucky circumstances.

Surfing builds confidence. It builds confidence in the beginning stages, when young surfers paddle through those lines of white water and make it out to the lineup on their own; when they have the control to sit on their surfboards without falling off; when they learn how to judge approaching swells; and when they finally catch a wave and stand up for the very first time. They gain more confidence in later stages as their experience grows; when they paddle into bigger surf; when they gain more control over their boards and master maneuvers like duck diving, aerials, or tuberiding. At every stage they grow physically stronger, and mentally more astute, and this builds confidence.

Whether facing a set wave at Pipeline or a potentially life-changing decision, I learned to take that drop with commitment. *I learned to trust in all the steps that have gotten me where I am. The result is that I feel better about myself,* and I have a lot of fun pushing myself into more challenging situations.

4

I Will Never Fight a Rip Tide

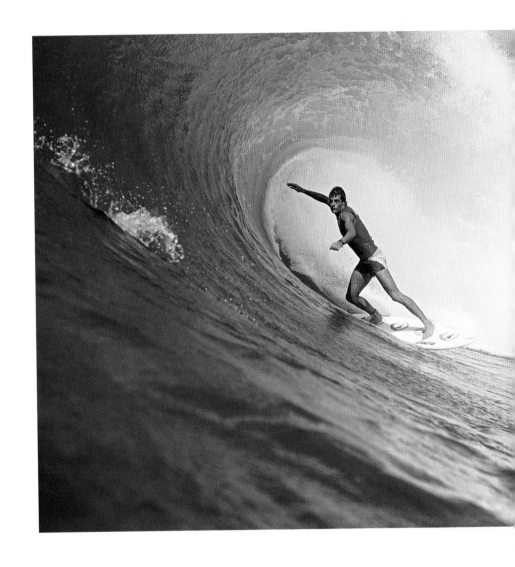

Straining to make the inside section at Sunset Beach, 1981 (photo: Don King).

When surfers sit on shore and watch the ocean, one of the things they are looking for is rip tides. Rip tides, as Willard Bascom will tell you, have nothing to do with tides. They are currents of water that flow out to sea, although not always directly. At the Bay of Plenty, when swells storming north from Antarctica produced especially pounding surf, we had a rip that ran parallel to the beach, about ten yards off shore, before turning alongside one of the jetties and running straight out to sea. At ten yards wide, surfers could jump into that rip on their boards, and the current would take them out to the break with their hair dry. *Surfers love rip tides. It is like stepping on a conveyer belt.*

Rips are only dangerous for swimmers who do not understand how they work. Trying to swim directly against a rip tide will wear a swimmer down, and many times the swimmer will drown. Surfers know the rule if they get separated from their board — swim out of the rip at an angle to the current. Even just floating on top of the water is better than fighting a rip tide directly, since rips normally dissipate once in deeper water, and the swimmer can then swim around the rip and return to shore. Surfers who have lost their boards will always head toward breaking waves because they know the white water will push them into shore. When faced with a more powerful force — and the ocean will always be more powerful than an individual — taking it head-on can be dangerous, even life-threatening.

I have two stories about surviving rip tides. The first time, I was able to think my way through the situation, and it saved my life. The second time, I allowed pride to interfere with good sense, and I stalled my surfing career at its peak for over a year.

The first story takes place at one of the most famous beaches on the North Shore of O'ahu—Sunset Beach. In my day, if you really wanted to gain a reputation as an accomplished surfer, you had to surf Sunset during a big swell, and you had to surf it well. Back then our surfing lives revolved around Sunset. We only rode the other spots on the North Shore when Sunset was not breaking. It was the ultimate big performance wave, the true test of a surfer's ability.

Despite all the excitement of tow-in surfing on the outer reefs of the Islands, *Sunset remains one of the most challenging big-wave spots in the world, filled with perfect, crushing waves.* Part of Sunset's special appeal is the history of the place, what the ancient Hawaiians called *Paumalu*. Legend tells of the Kaua'i chief Kahikilani who traveled to O'ahu to surf the famous waves of Paumalu. One day he fell in love with a bird maiden who invited him to live with her in a nearby cave. As time passed Kahikilani longed once more to test his skill in the surf; the bird maiden relented, but extracted a promise from the chief that he would not kiss another woman. When he unwisely broke his promise, he was turned to stone on the hillside overlooking the break and can still be found there to this day.

In the twentieth century, Sunset was surfed as early as the 1930s by young men—Whitey Harrison, Tarzan Smith, John Kelly—escaping the crowds at Waikiki and looking for more challenging surf. Sunset is still that way. Imagine an enormous field of water with endlessly shifting peaks, trade winds blowing hard into your face, crowds of surfers paddling this way and that, and one of the deadliest rip tides in the Islands. When the waves reach twelve to fifteen feet, which is about as big as you can ride the place, the rip runs like a raging river, cutting through the channel that separates Sunset from the next break over, a spot called Kammieland. ***The rip is so fierce that even on a surfboard you cannot paddle against the current.***

One late afternoon in 1974, the same year I started surfing Pipeline on Spider Murphy's board, I wiped out at Sunset and lost my board. In those days we did not have leashes, and after a wipeout one of two things would happen: either the waves washed your board all the way into shore, or the board ended up in the rip current and sailed out into the middle of the Pacific.

After wiping out, I took a quick look around for my board, hoping it might have popped through the wave. No such luck. So I began the long swim in — perhaps three hundred yards — constantly looking over my shoulder to dive under enormous waves. As I have said, surfers stay in the white water when they lose their boards. You never wanted to get caught in that rip at Sunset Beach. Ever. There was no way to swim against it, and you would get sucked out to sea and then have to swim all the way through the break again. ***In that size of surf, only the very strongest of swimmers can make more than one or two trips around the impact zone before getting completely worn down.*** Phil Edwards, considered the top surfer in the world during the 1950s and '60s, devotes a whole chapter in *You Should Have Been Here an Hour*

Ago to describing his rescue from the rip at Sunset Beach. And Phil was one of the best.

It was a long haul for me back to the beach, but I managed. I looked around and could not find my board...until I looked out to sea. Sure enough, it had gotten caught in the rip current and was headed straight out to the horizon.

Today, because boards are thin and break so easily, and because the top riders make quite a good living and travel with quivers of boards, a surfer would never do what I did, and that is to jump into the rip and swim after my board. We only traveled with a few boards back then, and we hardly made enough money to survive, let alone buy new boards. Honestly, when you found a board that finally worked for you, especially in competition, there was just no way you could let it go without a fight.

If I had been thinking straight, I would have remembered Phil Edwards' advice.

« You never wanted to get caught in that rip at Sunset Beach. Ever. There was no way to swim against it, and you would get sucked out to sea, and then have to swim all the way through the break again. »

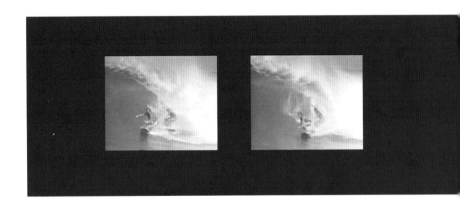

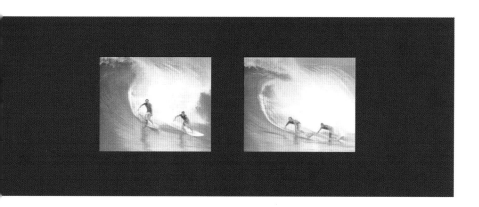

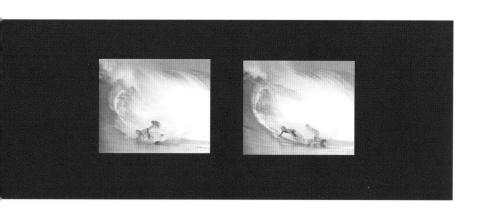

Segments from the film Free Ride *showing a once-in-a-lifetime wave behind one of the greatest surfers of all time, Mark Richards. Off The Wall, Hawai'i, December 1977 (a film by Bill Delaney).*

It was late afternoon, approaching sunset, but I dove into that rip and started swimming as hard as I could, powering along with the current, hoping to reach my board before it completely disappeared from sight. If I managed to retrieve it, the trip back to shore would be a fairly simple affair.

The channel at Sunset where the rip flows is quite deep. Because of the shark attack on my father, I suffered my whole life from an abnormal fear of sharks. It is amazing how vulnerable you feel swimming alone out at sea, in large surf, with the sky darkening. The fear is palpable. You taste it like you taste the salt water in your mouth. It was spooky for me to be in that channel, with water swirling around me. I was still in the rip, four or five hundred yards out to sea now, even farther than the first time I'd had to swim in.

My board, of course, was long gone, sucked out to oblivion. Now it was starting to get bloody dark, and I was all by myself, with fears of sharks circling beneath me. Even if someone had seen me in all that surf, it is unlikely a rescue attempt would have been made.

When I think back on the situation, it would have been so easy for me to hit the panic button. In fact, it would have been the most natural thing to do. The current ran fifty or sixty yards wide, rushing as fast as a man can run, and still pulling me out to sea. *I had to fight against my instincts to struggle, and my own personal fears.* I held onto the one thing in the world at that moment that could have saved me, and that was advice my father had passed on to me when I was nine years old: «SHAUN,» he said, «NEVER FIGHT A RIP TIDE.»

I held onto my father's advice like a life preserver. I waited until the rip released its grip, took a deep breath, and then started to swim toward land. Because I had not struggled in the rip, I had enough strength in reserve to make it through the most dangerous part of the break. *I got pounded all the way through the impact zone* and had to negotiate the edge of the rip the whole time to make sure I did not get sucked back out to sea again, but I kept my head and eventually made it to the beach — one board lighter, but a good deal wiser.

The second story takes place three years later and just down the beach from Sunset, at a break called Off The Wall. A little background information on Off The Wall: the wave sits right next to Backdoor which is the right-hand breaking side of Pipeline, the most famous and dangerous wave on the North Shore because it breaks in such shallow water. Like most breaks on the North Shore, it takes years of experience to pick the right wave at Off The Wall. The good ones give you a steep drop and incredible barrels; the dangerous ones close out over a very sharp and shallow reef. When the swell hits six to eight feet from the northwest, it strikes the reef perfectly, *creating intense tubes well-suited to my kind of surfing — high-powered ripping.* On some days Off The Wall doesn't even look like a spot at all, just a little piece of V-shaped reef, an afterthought. But on those rare days when the swell comes up slowly, around eight feet, the place really turns on, spinning deep, almost impossible tubes down the reef.

During that era all the best surfers in the world went down and surfed Off The Wall when the swell was too small for Sunset or some of the other spots to break. It was our unofficial gathering place during the winter surf season, the spot where everyone strutted their stuff outside of contests like the Pipeline Masters and the World Cup. It was actually more competitive than the contests. Without judges or points to worry about, each of us would try to *blow the other out of the water.* Because there was very little money in contests back then, we surfed for two things: press and prestige. A good reputation on the North Shore meant more than anything else in the world to us.

I had just won Hawai'i's biggest surf event, the World Cup. I had placed second in the Pipeline Masters, and I had won the World Title. I felt that I had cemented my reputation not only as the best surfer in the world, but also as the best tuberider. I had taken tuberiding to a different level, actually reinvented the way tubes were ridden, and I was surfing absolutely at my peak. I thought pretty highly of myself.

Mark Richards, an Australian surfer and a great rival of mine,

> « Because there was very little money in contests back then, we surfed for two things: press and prestige. A good reputation on the North Shore meant more than anything else in the world to us. »

came over to Hawai'i that winter with a brand new design called the twin fin. Guys had surfed on boards with two fins before. The earliest form of the design appeared in the late '40s and early '50s, created by an important figure in surf history, Bob Simmons. Simmons was a Cal Tech engineer who died tragically in a surfing accident in 1954, actually riding his twin fin. Some twenty years later, Mark Richards began to play with the design, tailoring it to match his particular surfing style and the changing formats of surf contests. Mark was a fairly big guy, and surfing on a single fin in small waves made him bog down. He realized that a twin fin would not only give him more speed, but given that contests were increasingly being held in small waves, a twin fin would make him much more competitive under those conditions. After he started *winning contest after contest* in 1979, the shape became extremely popular worldwide. Mark in fact surfed his new design to four World Championships, from 1979 to 1982, and twin-fin mania did not die out until fellow Australian Simon Anderson designed the three-fin thruster in 1981.

So, twin-finned Mark Richards and I were great rivals for many years. We were also good friends—not super-close friends, but good friends—and we had a tremendous amount of respect for one another in and out of the water. We shared some important commonalities. Both of us had fathers who were extremely devoted to our careers, and we each based our surfing around *power and carving.* We also felt that, no matter how well we had surfed in our respective countries, the North Shore remained the ultimate proving ground and that all our successes and awards were irrelevant unless we committed ourselves to ripping in Hawai'i at any spot, on any day, no matter the size or conditions. Off The Wall was the first place I saw Mark on his new twin fin design. He had already won the Smirnoff Pro in 1975 — held at Waimea Bay in large surf — and the World Cup that same year, so I knew he was a great surfer.

But I had won the title, and I had done it on a single fin.

The surf that day was three to four feet. I remember sitting on the beach with several friends, and Mark was out there lacerating waves on his twin fin. So I was looking at Mark surf the board, and suddenly it dawned on me: no way could I get that kind of acceleration on a three-foot wave with a single fin. I could see the future of surfing right there in front of me. I saw it in a second, but I was not willing to accept it. A huge rip tide started from the beach that day, and I fought it with hammer and tongs. *I let my emotions and my pride rule my decision making,* and for a whole year I fought switching over to twin fins.

A famous film sequence was taken of the two of us the very next day at Off The Wall. We were both riding the same wave, but I was farther back than Mark, and the story that has been told ever since is that I got the best of Mark Richards because I was riding deeper in the tube. He tried to cut me off, but I pulled up behind him and really showed him up.

Mark is not the type of guy who would normally drop in on someone, but I had dropped in on him earlier that day, basically because he had dropped in on me, although inadvertently I am sure. Most probably, he had not seen me. We were all trying to be the best surfer in the world, and in that type of highly-charged environment, things like that can happen.

Here is the version of that story that has not been told. That day in 1977 was the best day of the season at Off the Wall, and both Mark and I had been out in the water for hours. I had just won the World Title. All the best surfers in the world were either in the water or on the beach, and the sand was lined with photographers waiting to snap that classic cover shot. Dan Merkel, a water photographer shooting film for Bill Delaney's *Free Ride,* was floating in the impact zone with his camera. The vibe in the water was extremely intense, not aggressive in a negative way, but electric.

I was riding my favorite board—a 7'0 single fin—a tube-riding machine that my shaper, Spider Murphy, had made for me in South Africa. At the time single fins were the board of choice for the best surfers in the world. They were solid on the face and held a great positive line deep in the tube. I found that I could ride as far back as possible and sit the single fin right on top of the foam ball—compressed white water spinning up the wave face—and I could ride out the tube on my own little magic carpet. Suffice it to say that because of a number of technical innovations shaped into the board by Spider, *my single fins were the best, most sophisticated tube machines ever developed.* But in small, powerless waves they turned out to be real dogs because they lacked planing speed and acceleration.

So Mark dropped in on me. He probably had not even seen me, but on that day I was not going to cut him any slack. If you allow someone to drop in on you, and you do nothing, pretty soon everyone drops in on you. An hour later I returned the favor. I stuffed Mark in the pit, and he paddled back out absolutely fuming. Typically, if he saw me get a deep tube ride, he would counter with some incredible maneuver so that he would get the cover shot rather than me.

As he was paddling back toward me, the set of the day swung really deep into the reef, over toward Backdoor. I stroked into it, and Mark spun around. I was totally committed to the wave, and Mark fully intended to stuff me.

We took the drop side by side.

Mark delayed his bottom turn until the last possible second. I knew that I only had one chance: hit the turn perfectly and bring my board up into trim just slightly higher than his angle. Since Mark was on a twin, and I was on a single, I could hold a tighter line, closer to the wave face. I pulled the turn as hard and deep as I could, and right then the wave hit the inside reef and threw out. Generally the tube is a very solitary place, and until that moment I had never pulled into a tube behind someone. It was simply too risky. The chance of getting taken out by someone else's mistake was just too high. Even though I thought of myself as a radical surfer, I was still pretty cautious: I did not take off on closeouts, and I never tried insane maneuvers in big surf. As I pulled up behind Mark, the thought crossed my mind of bailing out, and then this sudden feeling of relaxation and confidence came over me. *There I was behind one of the greatest surfers in the world, and he was not going to fall.* The lip jacked up over both of us, and I managed to hold my line as Mark zigzagged through the tube in front of me.

And so the story goes that I got the best of him. I was Number One in the world, and I showed him up after he had tried to stuff me. *But the real story is that Mark got the best of me that day. The wave we shared was a turning point in the history of surfing.* Just as I had the technical advantage with my Spider Murphy board at Pipeline three years earlier, now Mark had the advantage with his twin fin. I might have been able to dominate at Off The Wall because the hollow waves were perfectly suited to my specialized equipment, but the writing was on the wall for single fins. Mark went on to change the way waves were ridden and to win his four consecutive world titles. That day ended the reign of the single fin, and I was not ready to accept it.

No board lost this time (unlike at Sunset Beach), but one that should have been—a single fin taken to the beach and buried in the sand.

The ocean constantly reminds us to be alert and to remain aware of our surroundings. It requires us to take the time to read signs so that we can anticipate potential dangers. Most of these signs are external—rip tides and impact zones. These are easy enough to spot and paddle around. Others are more obscure—internal ones like pride and stubbornness that can at times blind us to innovation and keep us mired in the past. The more we take to heart our own limitations, as well as our own potential, the more the ocean will increase our understanding of each.

5

I Will Paddle
Back Out

Edging around cyclone at Waimea Bay, 1981 (photo: Dan Merkel).

There are important stages in life that we are prepared to meet. They may be extremely difficult—leaving home, ending a relationship, changing careers—but at least we know they are coming and in some cases we have arranged them to take place at a certain time or on a certain day. We go into these situations with our heads up and our attention focused. Other situations we fall into accidentally, and these often reveal the most about our characters.

This lesson could just as well apply to pride, or lack of foresight. Either of these would work, but I would like to focus on perseverance. This is a lesson I learned about myself with the help of a wave that, until I actually encountered it, I had only met in my nightmares.

Most surfers know about the mysterious disappearance of Dickie Cross at Waimea Bay in 1943. Surf culture is filled with exciting and tragic stories, and this one is often repeated when surfers gather together. Cross was a teenager from Honolulu, an up-and-coming surfer at Waikiki who traveled out to the North Shore one day to ride waves at Sunset Beach with another surfer, Woody Brown. Brown, incidentally, built the first modern-day catamarans in the 1940s after working with ancient Polynesian designs. The North Shore was sparsely populated back then, and the two were among the first to surf Sunset Beach in the twentieth century. They would have been riding what is known as Hot Curls—finless, specialized big-wave boards—that weighed upwards of sixty pounds.

The two paddled into a swell that, unknown to them, was rapidly building. Soon the waves reached twenty feet and more. They were too big to ride, and the rip current at Sunset flowing too rapidly for them to paddle back to the beach. With the sun setting and the swell still rising, Brown suggested they paddle three miles down the coast to Waimea Bay. The two had passed Waimea on their drive out to Sunset Beach, and the protected bay looked like a good spot to get in safely.

It was dark by the time they arrived.

The swell had now grown so big that even Waimea was closing out—**_forty-foot waves crashing_** straight across the Bay. Brown and Cross had no other choice but to paddle through the impact zone to try and get into the beach.

In the darkness and the chaos of enormous swells, Cross lost his board and got swallowed up by a wave. Brown was luckier, and he timed his entry more carefully and washed into the beach half-drowned.

He never saw Dickie Cross again.

For many years afterward no one surfed Waimea Bay. Not only had Cross disappeared there, but the hill overlooking the Bay is hallowed ground for native Hawaiians. An ancient heiau or temple resides there, and the valley itself is an ancient burial site. The place developed an aura of danger and mysticism, and surfers stayed away. Then in the late 1950s, a small group of surfers decided to paddle out together on a medium-sized day. Suddenly, the tabu was broken. For the next forty years, until tow-in surfing came into its own, Waimea Bay remained the premier big-wave spot in the world. It was the Mount Everest of surfing, and if you had not scaled its summit, your reputation would never rank among the elite.

« The wave hit the shallow part of the reef and jacked up. The face went absolutely vertical on me. The board came completely out of the water, and I began free-falling with my arms stretched to the heavens and my toes barely touching the board, totally out of control. »

My first time surfing the Bay took place in 1975 during the final of the Smirnoff Pro Contest. Waimea needs a giant swell to work, and often weeks or even months can go by without a ripple at the Bay. So I had not expected to ride Waimea at all that winter. On this particular day an enormous swell had hit the North Shore; the Smirnoff started off at Sunset Beach, but the surf grew too big. Following in the wake of Woody Brown and Dickie Cross, the organizers moved the contest down the coast to Waimea, which holds a bigger swell. I did not even own a board big enough to ride the place, so I had to borrow one for the contest. It was a recipe for disaster. *My first time out at the most challenging big-wave break in the world, and I was using a board I had never surfed on.* Imagine Tiger Woods or Phil Mickelson breaking in a brand-new driver—no practice shots on the driving range—during the Masters; or Lance Armstrong pedaling a borrowed bike during the final leg of the Tour de France. The only difference is that a wayward slice or a sudden skid would not cost these athletes their lives. At Waimea Bay, this was a real possibility.

Conscious of the situation, I certainly felt apprehensive, but felt fired up as well. Money, reputation, personal pride, professional stature—all of these were on the line. I was twenty years old and it never crossed my mind that I might meet a wave so terrifying that it would *shake my confidence to the core.*

The first set I paddled into was pushing twenty feet, definitely a solid-sized wave. I wanted to pick off the first wave that came through just to get one under my belt: shake off the nervous energy, get used to how the wave broke, and most importantly find out if the board I had borrowed actually worked for me. I took a calculated risk and paddled farther to the inside—closest to the breaking wave—than all the other competitors. **It turned out my calculations were off. Way off.** I focused too much on getting that first wave and paddled too far to the inside. Not knowing the break at all, I did not realize I had placed myself into an extremely dangerous situation.

I remember catching the wave and standing up cleanly. As I dropped down the face I thought, «WELL, THIS IS PRETTY EASY.» I was about a quarter of the way down, knees bent, arms straight out in perfect balance.

The wave hit the shallow part of the reef and jacked up. The face went absolutely vertical on me. The board came completely out of the water, and I began free-falling with my arms stretched to the heavens and my toes barely touching the board, totally out of control. The board hit the bottom first, then I landed on the board and bounced off with so much force that my body began skipping across the surface of the water. Normally water is a soft cushion, but at high speeds it feels like asphalt.

The worst thing that can happen to a surfer who wipes out in big waves is to stay on the surface. It is critical to try and penetrate, or else the wave can land directly on top of you. Even getting sucked up the face and going over the falls with the white water — as gut-wrenching as that experience can be — is preferable to having the entire wave hit you squarely. When this happens a surfer can easily be knocked senseless, or even unconscious, and then drowning becomes a real possibility. The lifeguards at Waimea are the best in the world, but even for them a rescue in the impact zone is a tricky, time-consuming proposition. Donnie Solomon, a twenty-five year-old surfer from California, died in 1995 after trying to paddle through a set wave at the Bay. There was simply not enough time to save him once he went under.

That wave did hit me squarely. *I felt as if I had been walking along the highway and gotten hammered by a truck from behind — a terrifying impact.* Never to this day have I been struck so hard by a wave. It was a feeling of absolute crushing violence, an unbelievable sensation of force and power. I could not have imagined any human body taking such a beating and surviving.

The wave hit and took me down deep, too deep to see anything. Sometimes surfers open their eyes underwater, searching for those shafts of water illuminated from above that offer havens from the turbulence of breaking waves. In this instance it was completely black. I have never been especially conscious of the sensation of noise underwater, but as I was being plunged into this blackness, I heard pounding, horrifying noises coming from below, as great rocks rolled around on the ocean floor.

When I finally surfaced, gasping and coughing, I thought the wave had broken my back. I could hardly move my legs. My head felt as murky as those silt-filled waters back home in Durban.

We used no leashes back then. We had no caddies like pro surfers do today—guys who sit in the channel during a contest and can paddle over a replacement board. So I began to swim toward the beach. Slowly at first, then more desperately, constantly looking over my shoulders and trying to stay out of the rip, which would have sucked me out beyond the break.

I found my board floating in a deep spot about twenty-five yards

« Never to this day have I been struck so hard by a wave. It was a feeling of absolute crushing violence, an unbelievable sensation of force and power. I could not have imagined any human body taking such a beating and surviving. »

from shore. At Waimea the wave breaks a few hundred yards out, and then backs off over deep water before reforming into ferocious shore-pound. I hauled myself onto the board and looked first to the beach, then back to the lineup. I did not know it then, but *this moment turned into a defining point of my career.*

Twenty seconds of paddling, and I could have been safe on the sand.

But the contest was still running — guys scrambled out of the way as another set exploded off the reef.

I kept looking from the surf to the beach. I had just experienced the worst wipeout of my life, and I knew I could not survive another like it. The consequences of that moment meant everything to my career. At the time, of course, I did not even have a career in surfing since the World Tour did not begin until the following year. Yet for all of its importance, the action itself was so simple — *I swung my board around and paddled back out.*

Australian Mark Richards went on to win the contest. I rode a couple more waves in my heat, smaller waves than the one I had

> « Now if anyone had told me while I was getting
>
> mauled by that wave at Waimea that the
>
> business world would be a lot harder than surf-
>
> ing, I never would have believed them. »

wiped out on, and nothing worth going into detail about. Waimea taught me a critical lesson about positioning and perseverance. Never again will I make the mistakes I did that day. I had known after my wipeout that I was essentially done for the contest. I did not have to try to win after paddling back out, did not even have to surf my best during the rest of the heat. It was enough to know that I had turned my board around and faced those waves once again.

Now if anyone had told me while I was getting mauled by that wave at Waimea that the business world would be a *lot* harder than surfing, I never would have believed them. But after retiring from the tour in 1990 I had two devastating free-falls in business, both of which shook my confidence even more than the Bay. Yet *the knowledge that I did not give up on myself that day and take the easy way out has carried me through each crisis.*

The first occurred in 1995. I was sitting in the waiting room of a well-known apparel company in Southern California. It had not been my first job interview, and not even my second. What's more, I had never had to interview before because my whole life I had worked for myself. I had arrived that morning tens of thousands of dollars in debt after having closed the doors on my own apparel company in South Africa. Three years of hard work down the drain along with the dream of prosperity in and with South Africa. The consequences of going under at that point extended beyond my own survival to that of my wife, Carla, and my five-year old son, Mathew. After an extraordinary career on the World Tour as a champion surfer, as the owner of a successful apparel company that had sponsored other surfers, as someone who had always been optimistic and successful, I sat in that chair and realized that people had very little interest in Shaun Tomson. *Suddenly I was no longer a success,* and I was ashamed to go home.

I came from a family of successful entrepreneurs. My father and uncle both owned their own businesses, and my cousin, Michael Tomson — also a professional surfer — had founded the surf apparel company Gotcha in 1978. I followed suit in 1980 by founding Instinct. Even from the beginning of my surf career I had wanted to parlay my success on the Tour into long-term financial security in the business world. Instinct was created with this in mind, but after I retired from the Tour in 1990, I sold my share in the company after a dispute with my partners. Then I spent a year finishing my university degree in finance. Afterward, Carla — who earned a degree from London's Saint Martins College of Art and Design — and I decided to start over again in our native country. We called our company simply Tomson.

It was a personal and financial failure partially linked to the volatile times in South Africa. We were a country in political transition during those years, literally on the brink of civil war. Although the democratic elections in 1994 transpired peacefully in the end, the years leading up to the elections were extremely violent. The Natal area, which included Durban, had been placed under a state of emergency by President de Klerk. At stake, of course, was over three hundred years of white-dominated rule. Ultra-conservative factions among the Afrikaners had denounced de Klerk and fallen into league (amazingly enough) with equally radical elements among African militants. These forces had a vested interest in the failure of a unified South Africa, which would have meant a loss of independence for them. For the Afrikaners especially, a black-dominated government could mean retribution for Apartheid. So black and white fought battles in the streets against Nelson Mandela's African National Congress. To add to this chaos, South Africa had been in deep recession. Our business simply was not strong enough to survive such political and economic hardships. After three years of working and struggling I found myself in Southern California wondering not only about the future of South Africa, but, in particular, the short-term prospects for me and my family.

After the interview I was very shaken, not unlike the feelings I had experienced after my wipeout at Waimea, but more on an emotional level. I had a similar life-changing decision to make, but this time I understood, as I had not before, how serious the consequences of that decision would be for my family's future. Despite the shame I felt, it would have been easier to get on a plane and go back home to my wife and son rather than face another interview and risk those terrible blows to my ego. I phoned Carla in South Africa. Her advice to me was simple: «KEEP LOOKING FOR A JOB.» She knew—for the sake of my own self-confidence—that I had to find something, anything, before returning home. She was right, and I needed to have that reaffirmation from someone so important in my life.

I did paddle back out and find a job with a great clothing company, Patagonia, and then another one in the apparel division at O'Neill. After three years with those companies, Carla and

I decided to start our own company again, this time in Santa Barbara. We knocked on doors, talked about our ideas, and raised over a million dollars in investments. The apparel business is a demanding, time-consuming endeavor, and we could not have worked harder. Carla designed all the clothing and directed production while I oversaw the day-to-day business operations. After three years we had built up a great product line, with hundreds of distributors from California to New York. And then 9/11 hit, and the bottom fell out once again.

Our company, Solitude, experienced what many businesses did after the terrorist attacks: sales plummeted, and we had a hard time finding investors to recapitalize. Apparel is an especially expensive product to fund with a great outlay of time and capital on the front-end (to make the clothing) with the possibility of very little return due to changing trends, or even an event as unforeseen as the attacks on the World Trade Center. In essence, *I was looking at my second business failing in less than ten years.* We had no returns coming in to fund our next season, and investors were holding onto their capital until the political and economic situation stabilized. Overall, the situation was not unlike the turmoil leading up to the elections in South Africa.

On a Friday we began clearing out our offices in Santa Barbara — furniture, inventory, personnel. Everything except three things: my desk, my telephone, and my computer terminal. I had no idea what I was going to do come Monday, but as long as I had a phone hooked up I could still make calls.

It turned out I didn't have to. By chance one of my friends got talking with another father—Randy Paskal—at their sons' little league baseball game the next day. Randy and his father were looking for investment opportunities, and of course I was looking for investors. Carla and I met the Paskals the next day, on Sunday, and we shook hands on a deal. Monday morning, we started moving everything back into our offices. What is it they say in baseball? *It ain't over 'til it's over.*

We recently sold Solitude to Oxford, one of the largest apparel companies in the U.S., but Carla and I will still direct it. We face more competition now than I ever did in surf contests—and I certainly have gotten my fair share of poundings—but I have always made it back up. *Whatever comes over the horizon at me, I draw strength from knowing that my experience in the water supports other aspects of my life that now take priority.* I may still get worked over again in the apparel business and washed up on the beach. Home will always look like a comfortable place to rest and recover. But you know I'll be paddling back out again.

[LESSON]

6

I Will Watch Out

for Other Surfers

On this day, I finally broke my revolutionary pink banana, five years after it helped me break down performance barriers at Pipeline, 1978 (photo: Larry Pierce).

Surfing has the reputation of being an individual sport. Up to a certain point this is true. On a professional basis I have competed as an individual and gained individual honors. Outside of formal competition—and this comprises a minority of the surf population—most surfers prefer to seek out and ride waves alone, or with a few friends at most. I know I do. If surfing were a religion, the path to paradise would be built upon a personal relationship with the divinity. If surfing were a philosophy, enlightenment would be gained as the waves roll in, one at a time. Western culture idolizes individuals, and surfing itself, as part of that culture, has created its own heroes over the years. The sport's first hero in modern times was Duke Kahanamoku, whose imposing statue at Waikiki I have already mentioned. A native Hawaiian and Olympic swimming champion, Duke rode the biggest waves in the early part of the twentieth century. He helped popularize the sport by traveling around the world and holding surf exhibitions in places like Southern California, Australia, and New Zealand. When the world discovered Hawai'i as the ideal tourist location, **Duke was the official greeter—the Sheriff of Honolulu—**who introduced such celebrities as Charlie Chaplin, Bing Crosby, and Babe Ruth to the surf at Waikiki. From the 1920s to the 1960s, Duke was the face of Waikiki. The Duke's most contemporary incarnation, at least as far as notoriety goes, is Laird Hamilton. Laird is probably the best-known surfer in the world today. A big man who tows into the biggest waves, he has captured the popular imagination like no one else among his contemporaries. Duke and Laird also have something else in common—they both put their lives on the line time and again to save others in the water.

At its Polynesian roots, surfing is a communal sport, not an individual one. The Hawaiians held fiercely competitive surfing competitions each winter during the four months of the Makahiki festival, and although individual natives carried off the honors, by all accounts Pacific Islanders engaged in this activity in groups. Men, women, and children, commoners and royalty alike enjoyed and competed in the same waves for hundreds of years before contact with the first Western explorers in the eighteenth century. Reports from early travelers to the South Pacific record incidents of natives banding together during a surf session to drive off sharks and other predators. The Polynesians understood the old adage about safety in numbers. Then again, safety has not always been a surfer's top priority when it comes to riding waves, especially big ones. Surf culture has an interesting mix of the individual and the communal, and the two come together in a critical way when the waves are big and someone's life is on the line.

I can recall a lot of advice that I have collected over the years— *small shells of wisdom* given to me by people on beaches around the world that together form a valuable assortment of insights that I return to time and again to remind myself of what is important when I am in the ocean.

Growing up in South Africa, my friends and I were on the fringe of surf culture. The books and magazines that found their way to our shores were always out-of-date. We hungered for any news about surf-

« Even if surfers are out having fun for themselves

...inherent to the sport and to all good surfers

is accepting a degree of responsibility for other

people who are also out there enjoying the waves. »

ing from California or Hawai'i, and so before I actually had the opportunity to travel to such places, I had already read a great deal about
their history and traditions. One of the first writers I came across—
also one of the first to popularize surfing as something you could
actually do yourself—was Jack London. Not many whites practiced
the sport when London and his wife, Charmian, arrived in Waikiki in
1907. Hawai'i of that time also had a form of Apartheid, a highly
race-conscious society where a small minority of non-Hawaiians dis-
criminated against Asians and all but the most elite of Hawaiians.
London, a great adventure writer, recognized the inherent thrill of
surfing, and he was not above paddling out with the locals and learning the art of riding waves from them. It was an important moment
for the two cultures: Jack London, the rugged individualist, diving
into an activity whose traditions were essentially communal. But
when London wrote about his experience in *Cruise of the Snark,* he
had this to say about looking out for other surfers at Waikiki: «THE
SURF RIDER MUST TAKE CARE OF HIMSELF. NO MATTER HOW MANY

RIDERS SWIM OUT WITH HIM, HE CANNOT DEPEND UPON ANY OF THEM FOR AID.» We might have expected the author of *To Build a Fire* and *The Call of the Wild* to write something like that. London was a great writer, not a great surfer. It would be unfair to expect practical advice from him, but he did have an enormous impact on the sport. The strain of individualism he captured is so strong in Western culture that it takes a great deal of effort to counteract such bad advice.

In contrast, here is one shell of information that I picked up in Haleiwa, on the North Shore of O'ahu, in a surf shop, actually. Big-wave pioneer Fred Van Dyke, who was among that first group of surfers to break the tabu at Waimea back in 1957 and who dedicated the next twenty years of his life to riding huge waves, passed it along in his book *Surfing Huge Waves with Ease.* «IN HUGE SURF YOU SURF WITH OTHERS. YOU ARE DEPENDENT ON YOUR OWN ABILITIES TO SURVIVE, BUT ARE CONSTANTLY AWARE OF ALL WHO ARE OUT, MAKING SURE THAT THEIR HEAD POPS UP IF THEY WIPE OUT.»

Fred understands big waves as few people do. He understands how *the individual and the communal work together in the surf.* Even if surfers are out having fun for themselves, doing all those good things like building confidence and getting radical, inherent to the sport and to all good surfers is accepting a degree of responsibility for other people who are also out there enjoying the waves. Because the ocean will always be more powerful than the individual, we need to depend on one another. It does not take much time or effort, just a *simple acknowledgement of responsibility.* The rewards can mean everything in the world to someone in trouble.

The death of Mark Foo is a reminder of just how important our responsibilities are in the water. By the time he arrived at Maverick's, a surf spot in central California, in December of 1994, Mark had already gained a reputation as one of the top big-wave riders in the world. Raised in Honolulu, he had promoted himself as a professional surfer since the early '80s. Mark and I were not especially close, but we shared a desire to change the negative image that surfers had in society during this period. He took a lot of criticism for promoting himself. He hosted radio and cable TV shows out of the Islands and constantly wrote articles for the surf press about the specialized culture of big-wave riders within the larger culture of surfing. At the time, they were no more than a handful of dedicated individualists who mostly kept to themselves and liked to fly below the radar on the largest waves in the world. This was a decade before the emergence of tow-in surfing and before surfing big waves had really gained the popularity it now enjoys. He made famous the motto, «IF YOU WANT THE ULTIMATE THRILL, YOU HAVE TO BE WILLING TO PAY THE ULTIMATE PRICE.»

Mark paid that price in 1994. His death has become as legendary as that of Dickie Cross. He wiped out on a wave—not an especially big one by his standards—and he simply disappeared. His body was discovered only by chance more than an hour later. Maverick's is a very spooky place. "Cold Sweat," the *Surfer* magazine article that introduced the spot to the world in 1992, tells about Maverick's frigid surf, the dangerous rocks on the inside, and a ferocious top-to-bottom breaking wave. At least Waimea Bay has warm water and lifeguards.

No one knows exactly what caused Mark Foo's death, though drowning was the end result. There are large outcroppings of rocks underneath the lineup at Maverick's, and the most likely possibilities are that his leash snagged on one of them and held him under or his board hit him on the head and knocked him unconscious. It was the first time he had ever surfed Maverick's, so he did not know the break well. He had also paddled out after flying all night from Honolulu. *His death proved a deadly combination of ignorance and fatigue.* His reputation also played a part. Younger surfers were in awe of him and his experience at Waimea Bay. You might assume someone like that could look after himself. Certainly, his fatalistic motto did not help. They are not exactly words that signify caution or encourage others to cover your back.

All these reasons make the lesson resonate even more strongly. *If a wipeout can kill one of the best, most experienced big-wave surfers in the world, it can happen to anyone.* It is not just in big surf. Mark Foo's death was a tragedy that should not have happened. There were nearly twenty guys in the water at the time, multiple boats in the channel with photographers taking pictures, and great numbers of spectators on the cliffs watching the action. Ever since Maverick's had been exposed in the surf media, crowds of spectators and photojournalists stampeded to the break whenever a large swell registered on the radar screen. Maverick's was the first bona fide Waimea-sized surf spot in California, and no one had known about it. One surfer, Jeff Clark, had ridden the place for fifteen years all by himself, braving the cold water and remote location whenever the winter swells marched through. But by 1994 all that had changed. Incredibly enough, we have pictures of Mark Foo's last ride, even film footage. Yet no one in the water or on land that day made sure that his head popped up after the wipeout.

Looking out for one another **in the surf is a basic responsibility of all surfers,** from beginners to the most advanced, from those who ride knee-high waves to the guys who charge Jaws on jet skis. Every time I paddle out, I watch out for other surfers. I know that one day I might be in trouble, and I am going to be down there in the rocks running out of air, and I will be hoping there is someone above making sure that I make it back to the surface. Whether I am at Rincon surfing with friends, or off on a surf adventure in Indonesia with complete strangers, I always keep tabs on other surfers in the water.

I still try to read as much as I can about surfing, but because the roots of the sport are Polynesian and we remain essentially an oral culture, the best lessons are passed on through conversation. Talking story is one of the things that keep surfers connected to one another and to the waves. No book can take the place of sitting on the beach, enjoying a cool drink, and describing a surf session with friends. It is no surprise at all that *one of the most enduring influences of surfing on the larger culture continues to be our stories* and the language we use to embellish them.

The most compelling stories and videos coming out of surfing these days involve the tow-in crews. Surfers are riding waves verging on the hundred-foot mark, and they will break it as soon as a swell big enough rolls their way. Most interesting of all, these surfers have reinvented the sport as a team effort. In waves of that magnitude, safety is always at the top of their list. Never does a surfer assume that his partner will find his board or survive the impact zone on his own. The rider on the Jet Ski is constantly watching, and oftentimes there is a third person in the channel just for backup.

Laird Hamilton will tell you that he is able to catch gigantic waves because his partners, Dave Kalama and Derrick Doerner, are pulling him in and making sure that he makes it back out. Dave Kalama will tell you that when he has been plowed under by a fifty-foot wave and planted among the rocks and reef in the ocean depths, knowing that there are two guys watching and waiting for him gives him confidence to stay calm and make it to the surface. The only way these guys are able to push the limits of their surfing is because they place their lives in one another's hands.

I think few would choose to surf alone all the time. Surfers like to have other surfers around to share the experience and the stories. After fifteen years of surfing Maverick's by himself, Jeff Clark finally let his secret out to world. Why? He wanted to share the experience of this beautiful wave with other surfers. Thomas Farber, one of surfing's more thoughtful writers, describes common experience as one of the perks of surfing in his book, *On Water:* «THE PLEASURE OF A FRIEND'S COMPANY OUT ON THE WATER, SHARING BOTH EXHILARA-TION AND RISK, SHARING THE READING OF A GIVEN MOMENT'S OPTIONS, IMPERATIVES.» Beyond the option of which wave to pad-dle for and ride, and the imperative of how we spend our time in life, if I take responsibility to watch out for other surfers, I not only keep my friends around and keep those stories alive, but I go a long way to ensure that I make it back to the lineup for the very next swell.

7

There Will Always Be

Another Wave

Still trying to push my limits while approaching 50 at my adopted homebreak—Rincon, California, 2004 (photo: Glenn Dubock).

Localism and aggression in the water are hot topics of conversation these days. *Surfing is more popular than ever, and the waves are* getting crowded. One of surf culture's more prominent figures, 1966 World Champion Nat Young, got his face pounded black and blue by another surfer not too long ago while out surfing his home break of Angourie, Australia. The incident prompted him to publish a book called *Surf Rage,* and a number of socially-minded surfers contributed to the volume. One of them, Glen Hening, co-founded the Surfrider Foundation back in 1984 and—along with Matt Meyerson and former professional surfer Jericho Poppler—created the Groundswell Society, a grassroots organization that promotes social and educational issues related to ocean activities, and surfing in particular. I spoke at their annual conference in Ventura, and my success there inspired this book. Glen had originally asked me to tell a group of young people during a surf contest at Rincon what I have learned from the ocean. He told me to give them something they could take home with them. Rather than hand out a T-shirt or bar of wax, I decided to pass along the most important lessons of my career. I sat down and wrote them out very quickly, within perhaps twenty minutes off the top of my head. I printed them up on a card and handed them out that day.

So I am indebted to Glenn for the assignment. He is a teacher by profession. I think of him as the Jiminy Cricket of the surf world, with enormous reserves of energy and jumping from here to there, tugging at our collective conscience. If he sees a surfer he will invariably ask, «WHAT HAVE YOU DONE FOR SURFING? HOW HAVE YOU GIVEN BACK TO THE SPORT?» Hopefully, at some point in all of our lives, we are able to give back to those things that have provided us with enjoyment and educational experiences. Sharing these lessons with others has been one way for me to contribute.

Glenn, Nat Young, and the other surfers have written about violence in the line-up. It is true that really crowded surf breaks can be a catalyst for physical aggression, but it is certainly not inevitable. Sometimes we simply need to adjust our frame of mind.

Imagine this scenario. A surfer is sitting on his board in a crowded line-up. A wave rolls in, and he is in a position to catch it. Suddenly he turns to the man or woman sitting alongside him and says, «YOU TAKE THIS ONE.» What has he done? With four words he has immediately created a less competitive atmosphere in the surf, and most likely that surfer who enjoyed the wave will return the favor down the line, and pass a wave along to someone else. It is tough out in the water today. *We all get frustrated at crowded surf spots,* but it is easy enough to help create some unexpected good will in the water. *One thing I know—another wave will always come through.*

I surf on a consistent basis at one of the most crowded surf spots in the world, Rincon, in Southern California. I have mentioned that Rincon is a point-break wave. During the fall and winter, swells wrap around a point of land and break all the way down toward Highway One. When Rincon is firing, everyone within a hundred miles wants to catch a wave there. One morning during a new swell I hit the beach just as the sun was coming up. As I jumped into the water down by the Cove and started my paddle up to the point, I began counting heads.

I stopped when I reached two hundred.

Two hundred **surfers out at Rincon.** That is a fact of life in Southern California today, and in other areas around the world. We have to deal with the situation in a way that is not going to make us feel frustrated at the end of the day and ruin our surf sessions. Some people get angry in the water; they yell at other surfers, and sometimes there are altercations. Such scenes always remind me of Miki Dora at Malibu. Miki, who passed away recently, was the ultimate maverick in a sport that tends to collect such types. He had enjoyed surfing Malibu on a longboard in the 1950s, before crowds swarmed the place after *Gidget* hit the big screen and jumpstarted surfing's popularity into mainstream American culture. For a decade Miki fought the crowds at Malibu. He became a hero to some, railing against the exploitation of surfing by outsiders; to others he was a villain, aiming his board at surfers in the water and knocking them off what he considered to be his waves. It is a shame that someone with so much talent resorted to such base tactics.

He was fighting against *an inevitable tide* he could not stop. The tactics did not work in the long run for Miki. He could not fight everyone. He eventually gave up and had to leave the country. He spent some of his later life in South Africa, actually, surfing Jeffrey's Bay. I like to think that he learned a lesson from Malibu, calmed down, and enjoyed himself more.

For me, I would rather stay on the beach than surf in an atmosphere where people project such an aggressively narrow frame of mind. In fact, it does not have to be that way. If I tell myself before I paddle out that there will always be another wave or another surf session, then I know I have gone a long way towards making that surfing experience a positive one for myself and for the surfers around me.

I know from personal experience about violence in the water. Like Nat Young, I learned one of the most important lessons of my career by getting slugged in the face by an outraged surfer.

The incident occurred in the early '80s at Rincon, on one of the biggest days that I had surfed there. A big winter swell had rolled through, eight to ten feet in the bigger sets—a fantastic swell at a break that really suits my surfing style of broad carves on long walls of water. I remember paddling out and seeing this one guy fly by me on a wave. I said to myself, «ALL RIGHT, THIS GUY IS A GOOD SURFER.» In those days there were not a lot of really good

> « If I tell myself before I paddle out that there will always be another wave or another surf session, then I know I have gone a long way towards making that surfing experience a positive one for myself and for the surfers around me. »

surfers at Rincon. The place had dropped into a time warp of sorts. Many surfers rode longboards, which at the time was considered archaic. They wore black wetsuits and remained rather conservative. This was in part a reaction against the neon lifestyle that had taken hold a few hundred miles to the south in Orange County at places like Newport Beach.

The water was very cold. Often when the swell is big at Rincon, you have to wait a long time for the sets to come through. The swells are born from storms in the Aleutian Islands, off the coast of Alaska, and travel thousands of miles before landing on the shores of Southern California, so patience is a virtue. I had been waiting quite a while for a wave—long enough to start shivering a bit and for that good surfer I had seen earlier to finish his ride and paddle right up next to me. Sure enough, up popped a set.

I swung around and paddled for the wave. The guy had seen the set and also started moving. What he did was paddle around the back of me to get to the inside position. In South Africa we called this hustling. At other places they say "hassling" for a wave, or "snaking" a wave. *Where I grew up, a hustler was someone who always tried to paddle on your inside,* so this guy hustled me for the wave.

We both caught the wave. I saw him drop down behind me, and I made my bottom turn right in front of him, basically blocked the guy out of the wave and stuffed him in the pit. Why? Because it was my turn. I had waited like a gentleman, and he had taken the wave on the previous set. So I took this one. It was a late takeoff for both of us on a big wave, and he had a bad wipeout. I sailed all the way down to the Cove, a fantastic ride. I kept surfing for another few hours. I had recently come back from spending the entire winter in Hawai'i, so I was in great shape and quite used to surfing big waves.

Later that afternoon, I was sitting on the beach with my girl-friend at the time. We were hanging out at a low wall, just relaxing and chatting. Every once in a while a big set would roll through, and we would look out to watch the surf and the surfers. A guy walked up to me.

«HEY,» he said, «ARE YOU SHAUN TOMSON?»

Now ninety-nine per cent of the time when people came up to me on the beach, it was a positive experience. They wanted to meet me, shake my hand, or ask for an autograph. It always made me feel good. There are a lot of good vibes in surfing, and one of the best things about the sport is that the youngest grommet can sit in the water and share waves with the best surfer in the world. The only dividing lines in the sport are those created by Mother Nature.

I did not recognize him. He was not in his wetsuit, and he had several buddies with him. I guess I was not really paying attention.

He said, «YOU DROPPED IN ON ME.»

Perhaps it was the tone of his voice that tipped me off, but suddenly I realized what was happening. He stood with his fists clenched and his friends standing aggressively behind him. Now, I had been knocked about several years before by local Hawaiians on the North Shore for what they perceived as disrespect to them. My life had been threatened during that time, and at one point I had bought a shotgun because I had every intention of protecting myself if it came down to that. It never did, thankfully, but I had experienced much worse situations than this one. So I stood my ground. Later I found out that the guy had hassled other surfers before and been involved in a number of brawls on the beach.

«I WAITED FOR THE WAVE,» I told him. «YOU PADDLED STRAIGHT AROUND ON MY INSIDE. YEAH, I DROPPED IN ON YOU.»

He started yelling and cussing me out. I was not interested in dealing with the guy at all. I remember turning to the left to say something to my girlfriend, and *Boom! He slugged me straight in the face.* I was taken completely off guard. I jumped off the wall. He started throwing kicks at my head, martial-arts style, and his friends moved in.

The heavy cobblestones lining Rincon Point are the main reason why the wave breaks so well, and so consistently. Beach-break waves peel off underwater sandbars, which are always shifting around from storm to storm and season to season. But the cobblestones at Rincon are more or less permanent, and so the waves break in a very predictable pattern. This is great for practicing surf maneuvers. It is also convenient if you happen to need an effective projectile.

> « I think now that my complaint to the police was an important first step to changing people's attitudes about what is acceptable behavior in the surf.»

I was doing my best to block his kicks, and before the thing turned into an absolute brawl, I picked up one of the cobblestones and said, «ANY OF YOU GUYS COME CLOSE TO ME, AND YOU'RE GOING TO GET A ROCK ON THE HEAD.»

It was not an empty threat, but fortunately I did not have to heave cobblestones at anyone's head, and the situation diffused — with a bit more yelling and cussing.

Afterward I went to the police and filed charges. We both gave statements. Ultimately the District Attorney prosecuted the guy for felony assault, and they put him in jail. It was one of the first instances when a surfer had complained to the police about such behavior, which was more or less condoned in the surf community. Perhaps the DA acted on the complaint because I was a fairly high-profile person in surfing.

I think now that my complaint to the police was an important first step to changing people's attitudes about what is acceptable behavior in the surf. At the time I did not really care that they arrested him, or even convicted him. I wanted to forget about the whole experience. I surfed Rincon again, but not with the same enthusiasm. To have that sort of violence happen after a really enjoyable surf session really left a sour taste in my mouth. For months afterward I had the worst feeling in and out of the water just knowing that someone could lose control like that and actually slug me over a bloody wave. I left Santa Barbara not too long afterward to rejoin the world tour, and I did not come back to Rincon for a number of years, even though I loved the wave.

The guy was clearly in the wrong. He had not waited his turn in the line-up. He had paddled around me to get into the wave, and he had overreacted when he saw me on the beach. Of course our meeting was no chance encounter as he had seen me and waited for the most opportune time for the confrontation.

But what would have happened if I had let him *take that wave?* I would have waited—perhaps a few seconds, even a few minutes—for another wave in the set. I would have taken that wave into shore and probably gotten a great ride. I would have paddled back out and stroked into more great waves. I would not have been forced to fade the guy into the pit, would not have gotten slugged in front of my girlfriend and been part of an ugly scene on the beach. Most importantly, I would have enjoyed my next surf session at Rincon. *One wave is not that important, and there is always going to be another one.*

One day in 1955 at a surf spot on the North Shore called Haleiwa, a 26-year-old newcomer to the Islands named Fred Van Dyke stood on the beach watching wind-blown, ten-foot surf crash out at sea. A *haole* (pronounced *how-lee,* which means a white guy), Fred was anxious to paddle out and prove himself in front of a group of locals sitting in the shade and checking him out. The area was sparsely inhabited at the time—mostly plantation workers from the sugarcane and pineapple fields—and California surfers like Van Dyke had just begun to migrate over to the North Shore in search of its fabled waves. Haleiwa is still the hub of the North Shore surf scene, though these days you have to wade through art galleries and real estate offices before you get to the surf shops.

As Van Dyke tells the story in *Surfing Huge Waves with Ease,* one of the locals sitting in the shade that day was a Hawaiian named Henry Preece. A surfer himself, Preece had already befriended other big-wave hunters from California, surf legend Greg Noll among them. So as Van Dyke eyed the punishing waves and stressed over where to paddle out and how to line himself up for the surf session, Preece ambled over and offered him not only a cold beer but also some sound Hawaiian wisdom that so many visiting surfers over the years have learned to value, especially in a place as rugged and dangerous as the North Shore.

«HEY, HAOLE,» Preece said, «SOME DAYS FOR SURFING AND SOME NOT. THIS ONE NOT. HERE, HAVE A PRIMO. PLENTY MORE WAVES, RELAX.» Preece was generous to a visiting surfer—something we see less and less of these days—and the local knowledge that he passed along probably saved Fred a lot of headaches and possible injury that day. I don't think I can express the heart of this lesson any better than Henry Preece, so I will leave the last words to him.

Plenty more waves, relax.

{ LESSON }

8

I Will Always Ride into Shore

Redirecting back to the energy source. Off The Wall, 1975 (photo: Dan Merkel).

« Consider lulls. Surfers very reluctant, always,

to paddle in, sit waiting and waiting for one last wave.

Stare at the horizon as if able to will a wave

to appear, as if to turn for even a moment might

undermine the entire effort. »

THOMAS FARBER, *ON WATER*

How do I communicate my obsession? I am not sure the right words exist for such a project. I can state the physical reality of the situation plainly enough: for the life of me I cannot paddle into shore. Whenever I have gone surfing—from the time I was a boy until... well, the situation is ongoing—the time comes to finish the session, and *I have never paddled in.* **I have always waited for that last wave.** This can often take some time.

It seems silly, really. Why not just turn and paddle in? People are waiting, after all. On shore. At home. There is work to be done, appointments to keep and whatnot. Why sit hunched over in this binding fabric that never quite manages to keep out the cold, no matter how close-fitting against my skin? Why strain my eyes at a horizon slowly evaporating to darkness? Why tempt predators lurking in the depths with an evening meal of dangling surfer parts?

My answers only come in the form of questions. To understand why I refuse to paddle in, I find it helpful to examine why I have paddled out in the first place.

I get this sensation every time, driving my car along Pacific Coast Highway in the darkness of dawn patrol. I have already consulted buoy readings online and computer-generated forecasts, and yet that excitement pushing my foot deeper into the accelerator will not be justified until I top that last hill and actually see waves breaking in the morning light.

The sensation grows as I step onto the asphalt into brisk, off-shore breezes that lean against the waves, shoring them up with invisible shoulders just long enough for a surfer to slide quickly by and then, before relenting under the force of the oncoming swell and rushing out to sea, teasing delicate strands of spray from the wave's crown.

I walk along the beach now in the darker, hard-pack sand just below the high-tide line, my board tucked under my arm. The beach above the high-tide line is covered with dry sand. I see trampled husks of stranded jellyfish, still translucent but with no more substance to them than shedded snake skins. There are blackened bits of driftwood, broken shells, the stiffened carcass of a gull neatly camouflaged in an equally stiff and lifeless mat of kelp. The bright plastics are there, of course — rings, tops, fasteners, containers — all have become a natural part of beach landscapes across the world. The wind and sand will eventually bury or blow it all away, unless a higher tide takes them first.

Below the high-tide line, I pass clumps of seaweed teeming with beach flies and startle sandpipers nosing for crabs. I step over clam spouts in the sand. If my son, Mathew, were with me, he would scoop up shiny little rocks or shells he discovered, knowing they lose their shine as soon as he takes them from the water. All the animal life below the high-tide line jumps with urgency — birds, bugs, crabs — timing their movements with the constant sweep of surf and the approach of early morning waveriders. Anything not able to move under its own power radiates *life through color*, such as the deep reds and purples of kelp, and the vibrant green of delicate sea grass lying in single blades or tangled together like a mop.

On one knee, I wax the deck of my board — watching the sets

that come through, mentally timing them and waiting for a lull in the commotion—I jump off the sand into the water, and I float. I have jumped off the edge of the earth, and I am floating into a place of things unseen and waves rolling toward me that have yet to break, but I know they are on their way. It is an important moment, a split second of change from walking along the beach and existing in a world where I feel completely at ease to stepping into another sphere where I have so little control over what happens to me. To put it bluntly, I have now entered the food chain, and *while the risks are not ordinarily high, the potential for mortal danger is clear.*

I experience many stages as I jump into the water. First, the force and weight of my body on the board push me underneath the surface, then the air bubbles in my polyurethane board and my neoprene wetsuit raise me up again, above the surface, as if the water were pushing me away, resisting me. There is a sensation of weightlessness that tells

« ... a split second of change from walking along the beach and existing in a world where I feel completely at ease to stepping into another sphere where I have so little control over what happens to me. »

« When surfers make that leap from land to sea,

we pass through a threshold that changes who

we are and how we perceive the world. »

me that I am in a different place. After a few moments I reach an equilibrium in the water, and I stroke farther and farther from shore. *I get a sensation of wildness and wilderness. I have my back to the land, and I am looking out at a wild place.* Surfers practice this routine from ages ten through twenty, then we perform this ritual over and over until we are fifty, sixty, even seventy years old, and well beyond that in the case of surfing's most senior statesman, Woody Brown (the same Woody Brown who paddled to Waimea Bay with Dickie Cross in 1943). Woody began surfing in the 1930s and still has the stoke of a ten-year-old who has caught his first wave. David L. Brown's film *Surfing for Life* captures the joy surfing brings to the lives of men and women paddling into their eighth and ninth decades. It is true that riding waves will keep you young, even when you are ninety.

When surfers make that leap from land to sea, we pass through a threshold that changes who we are and how we perceive the world. That feeling is so special that when we have made the decision to paddle out, we know we have to leave that place gracefully and finish what we have begun. *It is not finished properly if we simply paddle in.*

When I first started on the World Tour in 1976, I was studying to be a lawyer (or an accountant, I had not quite decided) at Natal University in Durban. I had grown up in a Jewish household, and the expectations were that I would become a professional and follow the path of many of my extended family members. I never considered seriously that I could make a living from surfing until I actually started winning professional contests. The year before I had won events in South Africa (the Gunston 500) and Hawai'i (the Hang Ten Pro and Pipeline Masters) and probably earned about ten thousand dollars. The salary was not enormous by the standards of today's professional surfers, but at the time—and for someone competing only part of the year—the prize money got me thinking about a different career path.

But I was not yet ready to commit myself full-time to surfing. In 1976, a handful of surfers got together and formed a world tour, a grand-prix style circuit that would link together individual contests around the globe and crown an overall champion. Some thirty years later, this organization continues as the Association of Surfing Professionals, now based in Australia. I continued my studies at Natal University and again competed part-time. By year's end I ranked sixth in the world. This standing was encouraging enough for me to leave the university the following year and compete full-time on tour. That year I won the World Title. One contest led to another, each year followed the next, and I continued competing until 1989 and made a fairly good living.

Throughout my surfing career, I never went back to complete my university degree. I still had credits outstanding, and to me it always felt like unfinished business. Education had been important in my family, especially to my mother, Marie. She had strongly encouraged my studies from the beginning. I retired from surfing at the end of the 1989 season, and the following year Carla and I moved back to South Africa so I could finish my degree.

There I was again at Natal University, only it was sixteen years later and I was definitely the oldest student sitting in the classroom. Certainly I was the same age or older than a lot of the lecturers and professors who were my teachers. It was exciting to be in an academic environment again, a new challenge for me. The entire country seemed on the edge of something new and challenging. President F. W. de Klerk had recently assumed office and repealed the last of the Apartheid laws. He lifted bans against trade unions and political parties (including Nelson Mandela's African National Congress), suspended capital punishment, and freed political prisoners. Mandela himself walked out of jail that same year.

« That year I won the World Title. One contest led to another, each year followed the next, and I continued competing until 1989 and made a fairly good living. »

Amid all this inspirational change I had to force myself to complete papers and exams after having spent the past fourteen years traveling about the globe. I had an incredibly exciting year, but a tough year. I had a harder time than I'd imagined getting back that focus to do well academically. On top of all the political and personal changes, Carla and I found out that we were to become parents. Our son, Mathew, arrived in September, my final exams were set for October.

I could have decided to skip finishing my education altogether and go straight from professional retirement into a decent job in the surf industry. I would not have had to move back to South Africa or put myself through a whole year of taxing my brain in business classes. I would have been better off financially, at least in the beginning, and there were certainly no guarantees that a university degree would make much difference at all for my career. After all, the leverage I held in the surf world came from my reputation and accomplishments in competition, not from a university degree. My name alone would have carried a lot of influence in an industry that thrives on high-profile stars and personal connections.

« I could have decided to skip finishing my education altogether and go straight from professional retirement into a decent job in the surf industry... But it was unfinished business. »

But it was unfinished business. To me it was just the same as when the sun is fading and I am sitting on my board waiting for a wave. If I just paddle in, the session doesn't have as much significance. Each and every surf session is special, and *it is important to finish things properly, end on a good note and catch that last wave in.* There is no reason to rush what need not be rushed, or to bring premature closure to something so satisfying.

No one is going to know, really, whether I catch that last wave in or not. Many of the lessons here have importance for other surfers in the water, either in terms of safety or courtesy. But this lesson— *whether to paddle or to ride into shore—is a personal decision* that comes from the inside for no one's benefit but my own. This one I do for myself.

I Will Pass

Along My Stoke

Feeling the stoke at Backdoor Pipeline, 1976 (photo: Steve Wilkings).

One word defines the essence of surfing better for me than any other—stoke. I do not know how or when the expression was introduced into surf culture, but that image of a fire being stirred up in the pit of one's stomach captures the feeling surfers get when they see good waves or surf a great session. Unlike other expressions that began in surf culture, stoke is still fairly exclusive to surfers. You do not hear it much from people who do not surf, so it retains that unique quality within the culture.

One of the best things about stoke is that you can pass it along to someone who has never heard the expression. I have taken beginners out surfing and noticed that even before they have the vocabulary to express their joy, *I can see the stoke in their eyes and in a smile that burns as bright as a bonfire.* Push them into one wave and watch as the surf speeds them to shore; their exhilaration comes from the wave itself as it crashes and transfers that pent up energy into their body skimming along the surface.

In one particular case this happened with a guy I met through my business. I come into contact with many different people on a daily basis, most of whom do not surf. My 45-year-old acquaintance had always heard about the sport, of course, and wanted to try it for as long as he could remember. He learned that I surfed, so one day he asked me.

«SHAUN,» he said, «I'D LOVE TO GO SURFING SOMETIME.»

«C'MON,» I told him, «I'LL TAKE YOU OUT.»

There is no better feeling than getting another person stoked on surfing. Truly, it does not bum me out that there are more surfers in the water these days. It just means that I have to get up earlier in the morning. When I saw this man rise on a wave for the very first time, I felt as if *I* had gotten up on a wave for the first time again. He hollered so loudly his voice echoed off the cliffs lining the beach. It is a precious thing to see a middle-aged man as excited as a child. The ability to tap into primal emotions is certainly one of the enduring gifts of surfing. Although surfing has been portrayed for many years as a sport for young people, the youthful part of riding waves is not the age of the surfer but the feelings that surfing produces. ***Passing along those feelings — that stoke — brings people young and old together*** like no other activity I can think of, and it basically works like trust because the more you give, the more you get back.

If riding waves is the lifeblood of surf culture, then stories are the heart that keeps that blood pumping. Surfing is not a sport where you can shoot eighteen holes, record the numbers on a piece of paper,

« Although surfing has been portrayed for many years as a sport for young people, the youthful part of riding waves is not the age of the surfer but the feelings that surfing produces. »

then go back the next day and play that exact course again for a better score. Once you have ridden those waves, they are gone. *All that remains is a trace of salt on your skin, a feeling of contentment in your soul, and a story or two.* I have mentioned that surfers form part of an oral culture, which we have picked up from the Hawaiians. Every person should spend at least one summer evening at Ala Moana beach on the south side of O'ahu, relaxing on the grass after a surf or swim, watching the sun go down, feeling the trade winds cool your skin, and listening to the locals tell stories. Not epics, not big dramas, just everyday stories. The most extraordinary experiences surround surfing, and many of them have little to do with actually riding waves. Here is one that always comes to mind when I think about passing along stoke to another person.

I have given surf lessons to my son, Mathew. He is interested in surfing. He is not obsessed with it as I was at his age — at least not yet — but we certainly paddle out together as often as possible. The closest break to our home is Hammond's Reef, a beautiful little beach that is typically uncrowded because of its secluded location. We usually park and follow one of the paths bordered with ice plant to a bench that sits on a grassy knoll overlooking the point. Behind us rise the wooded San Ynez Mountains filled with trails for hikers and bikers. Before us lies the beach itself, layered with gray cobblestones that range in size from softballs to watermelons and larger. Great tangles of driftwood gather at the high-tide line, cast ashore by winter storms.

From the bench we can spot swells rolling through and also the remains of campfires among cobblestones that visitors have dragged into rough circles. Mathew and I have our particular stones along the path underneath which we stash our bars of surf wax in case the swell is up and we decide to paddle out. When the waves are quiet and the wind dies down, the whole atmosphere at Hammond's is calming. *We hear the rhythmic sound of the waves and watch the sun glint off the surface of the water, which resembles a field of sparkling diamonds. Sparkle factor* is the expression surfers use to describe this condition, and it reminds me of why I chose to live and work in Santa Barbara.

So Hammond's is a special place for me because I share it with my son. Beyond a touch of serenity in an otherwise hectic world, Hammond's is also home to a Chumash Indian memorial. Much of the coastline in this area was peopled by the Chumash. They thrived here thousands of years before the missionary period in the late 1700s. Places like Hammond's and Rincon served them as protected bays where they could launch their canoes in safety, and they used the natural tar seepages in the region to seal their small ocean-going crafts. About half a dozen years ago Mathew and I were walking along the beach at Hammond's just checking the surf—Mathew was nine at the time—and he suddenly said, "Let's go up and visit the memorial."

The memorial sits in Shalawa meadow, a small clearing just south of the grassy knoll and back from the beach a ways, no more than a few minutes walk. The cobblestones along the shore give way to scrub brush and large rocks that are havens for lizards; gopher holes dot the meadow here and there, and the monument stands right in the middle

My son Mathew and I enjoying a special moment at Hammond's Beach, the site of the sacred-story circle (photo: Bruce Weber, beach photo: Jeff Novak).

of the clearing. It is four or five feet tall, rectangular in shape, and covered with decorative tiles on the side that faces the Pacific. Between a couple of dolphin figurines are composed the following words:

The sacredness of the land

lies in the mind of its people.

This land is dedicated to

the spirit and memory of

the ancestors and their

children.

Around the base visitors have left various rocks, shells, flowers, and driftwood, all pulled from the beach and set in a semi-circle so that the memorial also has the feeling of a small shrine. With the mountains rising behind the meadow, and the Pacific stretching out as far as one can see, the area has that dramatic quietude common to ancient and spiritual places. One cannot help but think of all those who lived and enjoyed this terrain over the centuries — families, fishermen, entire communities — and all the people in centuries to come who will enjoy this meadow, drink in the Pacific vista, and pay their respects to the land.

After Mathew and I spent a few minutes gazing at the memorial and added our own offerings, we walked back to the beach. «DADA,» he said, and that was what he called me when his friends were not around. «HELP ME DO THIS.»

He started to pick up cobblestones, one at a time, and arrange them in a large circular shape right on the sand. «WHAT IS THAT YOU'RE MAKING?» I asked him. He did not answer, but kept adding stones to complete the circle. I began to help him without knowing why, simply because he asked me. Once we completed the circle, Mathew began to make a smaller one inside of the first, again by hauling over cobblestones some of which would have broken his foot had he dropped them. I followed along, walking here and there for likely-looking stones and carting them back. Once we completed the second circle, Mathew began to form yet another one inside the other two. He still had not told me what we were doing, but I continued to help. By the end we had three concentric circles of stones on the sand. Mathew got down on his knees and shifted several of them around to form an entryway into the very center. Then he left and grabbed two rocks, one at a time, to serve as our seats.

Once he had done that, he straightened up and scampered down the beach.

«HEY,» I called after him, «WHERE ARE YOU GOING NOW?»

He did not answer but continued down the beach to a pile of driftwood. He pulled out a small stick, and then began looking around on the ground. As it turned out, he was searching for feathers, probably from a seagull. He then pulled up a small strand of kelp and wrapped it around the feathers to attach them to the wood. I stood and watched as he brought the whole mess back.

«WHAT ARE YOU DOING?» I asked again.

«IT'S A SACRED-STORY CIRCLE,» he said.

«TELL ME ABOUT IT.»

«WHAT WE'LL DO,» he said, «IS TELL EACH OTHER STORIES INSIDE THE SACRED-STORY CIRCLE. WHEN YOU'RE TELLING A STORY, YOU HAVE TO PASS THE STICK TO THE OTHER PERSON.»

«ALL RIGHT,» I said.

So we sat there together on the beach. It was the middle of the morning and no one was around, and we passed the stick with the feathers and the kelp back and forth and told each other stories. We just made them up. I hardly even remember what we said, but we must have sat there for at least an hour. When I think back on the whole scene, I am amazed. I sat in the sand with my nine-year-old son, and we told each other stories inside a sacred-story circle. At the time I did not make the connection between what Mathew and I were doing and the inscription on the Chumash memorial which links us to the past, to the land, and to our children. I was simply following along with his little game. But the special atmosphere of Hammond's Reef itself—the secluded beach, the mountains and the meadow, the small rocks and shells and feathers that visitors leave at the base of the monument as a tribute—all of it has worked on my imagination and memories over the years so that *I have come to appreciate that one hour more than almost any other time I have spent at the beach,* including innumerable surf sessions at the most famous breaks in the world. Mostly, I think, because it was an experience that I did not expect to have, and one that has become inseparable from a special place and special person in my life. The combination of the grounds where I sat and the presence of my son connected me to something altogether larger than myself—to the past and the land itself, to the future embodied by Mathew—and that has resonated strongly with me ever since.

Hammond's is our local break, no more than a five-minute drive down the hill. Mathew carried a small cobblestone back with him, one that he had taken from the innermost circle. He set it right outside our front door.

«WHY DID YOU BRING THAT HOME?» I asked him.

«YOU KNOW ALL THOSE STORIES WE TOLD TODAY, DADA? THEY'RE ALL INSIDE THAT STONE.»

The sacred-story circle and the sacred-story stone. *I have never been so stoked in my life.* When we had left that morning to visit Hammond's, *I thought that I was passing along stoke to my son* by visiting the beach and maybe giving him a surf lesson. Little did I realize the gift that he had in store for me, one that I enjoy every time I think of Hammond's or look at the sacred-story stone outside my front door.

10

I Will Catch a Wave

Every Day

Super Tubes, Jeffery's Bay—my favorite wave in the world, July 2005 (photo: Joli).

Some of the best surfers today are in jail.

They slouch on bunks hour after hour and project their imaginations against cold concrete walls that suddenly fold into liquid blue ones. They stare for days on end at lines stacked *vertically* — ruler-edged, wrought-iron bars fill their horizon — and they dream of riding waves. Surfers have a special term for this. We call it *mind surfing.* You can mind surf a wave as you stand on the edge of a cliff and watch a swell march into your local break. You can mind surf a wave sitting behind your desk in school or at the office. If you have surfed long enough, mind surfing kicks in automatically when your brain starts to combust from the pressures of daily life. It is like air conditioning for the spirit, only more refreshing. Every so often the surf magazines will publish a letter from one of these prisoners who is sending out a word of warning to other surfers: *Stay off drugs,* or *Don't mess up your life like I did.* It may be too that the prisoner is just trying to make contact beyond the cellblock. Some bloke locked up rather than locked in, who cannot get to the beach and is now forced, calendar to calendar, to replay that one session over and over in his mind. Having been raised in South Africa under Apartheid, I am always reminded of Nelson Mandela when I read such letters. Twenty-seven years in prison. Imagine what the walls of his cell looked like as his imagination played against them. Or Henry David Thoreau, whose nonviolent resistance landed him in jail and ultimately influenced both Gandhi and Mandela. «AS THEY COULD NOT REACH ME,»

Thoreau wrote, «THEY HAD RESOLVED TO PUNISH MY BODY.»
Thoreau recognized that his ideas were much more dangerous than
his person because they could not be silenced or sentenced away.
Mandela must have drawn strength from Thoreau and others whose
imaginations skipped—surfed, we might say today—beyond the
confines of prison bars.

I find that society encourages us these days to compartmentalize
our lives. We have our work and our pleasures, and the two do not mix
readily enough. I will not go so far as to say work is like prison, but
there is a forced confinement there, even if a self-imposed one, that
should not have to come at the expense of our imaginations. The two
can be absolutely compatible. There are some days, for example, when
I do not even see the beach let alone paddle out for a session. I have
my business, my responsibilities, and so it is important for me to find
a way to bring the beach into my life, even if only for a few moments.
The best part is that *mind surfing is not an escape
from work—it helps me work better.*

I need surfing now more than ever before. Since Carla and I
started our apparel business in Santa Barbara, it seems all I do some
days is sit in my office and stare at marketing proposals.

Once in a while my head will drop straight down onto my desk.
*Man, it'd be just great to paddle out and get
one good wave,* I think, then close my eyes and the frames
start clicking away.

I am back home in Durban, South Africa. I feel the cold sand
under my feet and a stiff offshore blowing at my back. But the sand
and the wind are not what is giving me goose bumps. It is 1974, and

I am staring at a new swell pounding the Bay of Plenty.

I lean down on one knee and start rubbing wax into the deck of my board, making steady circular motions from tail to nose. My heart pounds with every wave that detonates off the sand bar, and I know that I am either going to get the ride of my life today, or I am going to wash up on the beach with a broken back. I stop waxing and look up and down the beach. No one is around.

So I have a decision to make. How badly do I really want it?

Just those few moments give me a wonderful, vicarious feeling. My blood is pumping again. I lift my head off the desk, for I am refreshed and ready to tackle those spreadsheets.

All surfers have one special wave they recall vividly. Go ahead and ask sometime. You will get an instant smile, a shake of the head as if they still cannot believe that it happened. They will begin to describe random details—how cold the water felt that day, the color of the sky, the sensation of wind on their face as they dropped wide-eyed into that one miracle wave. Because words are not enough to convey the full experience, surfers begin to move their hands and bend their bodies this way and that as if to conjure that wave and that moment back to life. If you saw them from a distance, you just might think they were casting a spell. A surfer will be standing in front of you and talking, but his eyes or her voice will tell you they are locked in a wave miles, perhaps continents, away.

I have had many great surf sessions during my professional career. I have been fortunate to ride swells at Jeffreys Bay at the tip of South Africa that lasted so long my legs gave out. I have surfed Pipeline, on the North Shore of O'ahu, at its very best, and Sunset Beach, also on the North Shore, at its most dangerous. Let me take you back to

Durban, 1974, and the *single greatest wave* of my life. I say greatest not so much because of its size or shape, though certainly both were memorable, but in the particular way this wave tested my imagination.

A good south swell had hit the Bay of Plenty, which is the best swell for the Bay. A real gloomy day late in the afternoon, dead low tide. We used to get very low tides at certain times of the year in Durban. Storm systems from Antarctica pounded the beaches in the wintertime and created a ferocious riptide that ran along the beach and dumped truckloads of sand at the end of a jetty where it formed a tremendously long sand point. There is not much resistance from the continental shelf in this part of Africa, so the waves roll in very fast and very strong. On this particular day the swell was so big, and the waves sucking so strongly off the bottom, that a surfer who managed to catch a wave would actually be riding below that sand bar, below sea level.

I had brought a longer board than usual to the beach, a 7'7" that I normally only rode in the Hawaiian Islands on a big day. As I sat on

« Just those few moments give me a wonderful, vicarious feeling. My blood is pumping again. I lift my head off the desk, for I am refreshed and ready to tackle those spreadsheets. »

the sand and watched wave after wave pound the shore, I honestly did not think the swell could be surfed. The waves were simply coming in too fast and breaking in too shallow of water. But every so often a wave hit the sandbar and peeled perfectly. A freight train, certainly, but one I might manage to hang onto with the longer board. Now *if I committed to the wrong wave, I would get driven head first into that sand bar.*

But if I picked the right wave . . .

I jumped into the riptide, knowing there was only one way back to the beach. As soon as the rip pulled me beyond the jetty, I began to prowl the impact zone. I paddled for a wave, then backed off. I paddled for another, backed off again. It was extremely frustrating. I had so much adrenaline pumping through my body. I wanted to catch a wave, but I had to consider the possibility that I had been right after all, and the swell simply could not be surfed.

As I sat and mulled this over, rising and falling with these enormous swells surging underneath me, it occurred to me for the first time that *I would not be able to tell which wave was going to hold up until I had already dropped down the face.*

«TO HELL WITH IT,» I said finally, and I kicked into a big one.

At this extreme low tide, a lot of sand was sucking up the wave face. As I pulled my turn on the bottom and looked down the line, I thought I had just made the biggest mistake of my life. The wave looked like a sand cavern, only it was moving fast and now closing down on top of me. I could have bailed out right then, tried to use the momentum from my drop to punch my board through the back of

« I was in a dangerous position, racing high on the wall right over the sand bar. If my board had been any higher, my single fin would have spun out of control. The section of wave ahead was mindless and walled up as far as I could see. No chance of escape at all. »

the wave. I might have made it.

I will never know.

I had one line on that wave, and one line only, and I held onto it. It grew dark inside, and this is where I lose track of what happens exactly when. I saw an eye of light at the end flashing open and closed, now giving me hope, now shutting it down. I remember focusing on that tiny portal as it telescoped farther and farther away from me. I was falling, at that point, farther and farther back from the light, getting sucked back into the tube, and I thought, I'm not going to make it now. I'm too far back.

I was in a dangerous position, racing high on the wall right over the sand bar. If my board had been any higher, my single fin would have spun out of control. The section of wave ahead was mindless and walled up as far as I could see. No chance of escape at all.

In these extreme situations there is always the tendency to jump. Just bail off the back of the board and throw your arms in front of your face. Take the hit you know is coming. And sooner rather than later, because more speed is only going to make things worse. At least you have chosen the moment, right?

It is fear that tears us down, and lack of imagination: I can't keep this pace. I can't ride any deeper. It's not possible to go any faster on a surfboard and survive.

If I had had the slightest cushion of water beneath me, I might have jumped.

Suddenly I heard the wave explode behind me. All this spray flew past—I felt it drive into my body like a gale—and it blew with such force that it actually lifted the board right off the water, and me with it.

My board and I were flying along completely out of the water now, inside the barrel, carried along by this blast of supercompressed air.

> « I was flying along in almost complete darkness
>
> with the wave breaking around me in slow motion.
>
> Suddenly the board dropped back down onto
>
> the surface of the water, and I came flying out
>
> of the barrel into daylight. »

I was twenty or thirty feet back in the barrel, with this amazing sensation of flying through the air on a surfboard.

Many surfers will tell you that at certain times in the tube, at critical high speeds, they experience the sensation of the wave moving in slow motion. The body is reacting to danger. When you cannot fight, and you cannot run, the senses go to red alert where every nerve becomes a seismograph, registering and reacting to the slightest shift in the immediate environment. In this altered, hypersensitive state of mind and body, the wave actually appears to churn in slow motion. The result is that you feel like you have *all the time in the world* to react. Adjust your stance, dodge the lip, shift your weight forward or backward, carve up and down the wall, anything that allows you to maintain your line and keep from getting crushed. The sensation is as palpable as a clenched fist.

I was flying along in almost complete darkness with the wave breaking around me in slow motion. Suddenly the board dropped back down onto the surface of the water, and I came flying out of the barrel into daylight.

No spectators were screaming on the beach, and no voices droning point totals over the PA system or camera shutters clicking away. I heard only the sound of the wind. And as I drifted over the shoulder, I looked back down to where I might have been. How thin that line is between doubt and imagination, between getting the blade of the axe or the handle.

Every surfer has a similar story. One moment they are being dragged into oblivion, the next they are flying along on the very breath of the wave. *The feeling of time being expanded and distorted, of fear and exhilaration all melded together,* these are rare sensations that replenish the spirit and sustain the soul.

A well-known poem by William Butler Yeats hangs above my desk at work, and I look at it every day: *An Irish Airman Foresees His Death.* The last four lines have always reminded me of that wave at the Bay of Plenty:

> *I balanced all, brought all to mind,*
> *The years to come seemed waste of breath,*
> *A waste of breath the years behind*
> *In balance with this life, this death.*

I have so many associations when I read these lines: the sensation of flight, like the airman in the poem; the breath of the wave; the sense of danger; the commitment to fly in the face of that danger; and the importance of balance and imagination. Over all of these is the ultimate decision to *live in the moment and to choose one path and follow wherever it takes me.* That path is not a destination, which surfers are never concerned with while on a wave, but *simply living with passion.* I gain an enormous sense of calm knowing that I chose a path not for prize money or the accolades of others, but for what Yeats terms «A LONELY IMPULSE OF DELIGHT.» In the end I followed my passion.

I see a complementary relationship between our actions in life and our imaginations where each defines, and is defined by, the other. This holds true for my surfing. The more I surf, the more possibilities open up to me, and the more possibilities I can imagine, the better my surfing becomes. And the richer the entire surfing experience.

Because surfing stays with me after I leave the waves — in the salt on my skin, the pleasant ache in my shoulders, that general sense of well-being that warms my whole body like a summer day — *I can draw on those physical sensations to nourish the imagination and invigorate my life every day.*

[LESSON]

11

All Surfers Are Joined
by One Ocean

Carving back into the curl at the infamous Sunset Beach on an early '80s version of Simon Anderson's invention, the three-fin thruster (photo: Dan Merkel).

There is no getting around it: as soon as you have paddled out and caught a wave—even a small one, perhaps only one in your life—you are a surfer. At least at heart. *Surfers have a commonality of experience that is special. We are different from other people,* and different things motivate us. Many years ago, 1966 World Champion Nat Young remarked that *all surfers form part of a tribe,* and he was right. Our shared language is often primal, expressed in hand gestures or the hoots of approval we direct at complete strangers while paddling out. We have our rites and our rituals: dawn patrol, for example, when surfers rise at first light filled with that eternal hope each new day always brings—in our case the hope for waves lined to the horizon; and the *ho'okupu* ceremony, when surfers gather in a circle at sea and bid farewell to other surfers who have fallen. These traditions form part of a common language that bonds surfers to one another all over the world. We may ride waves in waters with different names—the Pacific Ocean, the Atlantic Ocean, the Indian Ocean, the Irish Sea, the Mediterranean, the Bay of Biscay—but even a child will tell you that if you look at a globe, there is really only one ocean. *I prefer to look for ways to connect with other people* rather than to focus on differences. I do not deny difference—I respect it, but I like to work toward commonalities. How else could South Africa have come together as one country if two men from such diverse backgrounds as Nelson Mandela and

Frederick Willem De Klerk had not reconciled their differences and worked toward a common goal?

Here is a crash course in surf meteorology. Swells are born in the Aleutian Islands off the coast of Alaska in the wintertime — formed by the clash of temperatures around the Arctic Circle — and they radiate across the Pacific Rim to the Americas, Japan, and Australia. As the seasons change this global flow reverses and storms from Antarctica roll into the northern hemisphere from the south and touch every shoreline like ripples in a pond. *The energy that moves across the ocean connects all surfers who ride it.* Many surfers will travel with the swells, sometimes great distances. One can ride waves in Tahiti, hop on a plane to the Hawaiian Islands and enjoy waves from that very same swell, then take another flight to California — heading ever north — and slide in the surf once again along the shores of the Golden State. All that from a single storm. One surfer connects with a swell in many different places, and one swell connects many different surfers all in those same places. This shared energy gives surfers a commonality of experience. The history of surfing shows that riding waves has crossed great spaces and cultures, from Tahiti to Hawai'i to North America to Australia and back again to

« We may ride waves in waters with different

names... but even a child will tell you that if you

look at a globe, there is really only one ocean. »

Tahiti. One of the heaviest and most photographed waves in the world today, Teahupoo, sits off the south end of Tahiti, not a great distance from where Captain Cook landed in 1769 on his first voyage to the Pacific, a trip where his crew members recorded local Tahitians body-boarding waves in Matavai Bay. So across countries and cultures surfers are connected not by nationality or religion or politics or age or sex but by their experience riding waves. This is a *powerful experience* both in the waves themselves and inside each surfer.

That is the bigger story of how surfers are connected. A much smaller story I would like to tell is how one particular surfer has had—and continues to have—a daily impact on nearly every surfer around the globe today, from the youngest grommet to the most senior members in lineups from Malibu to Mozambique. The surfer's name is *Simon Anderson, the inventor of the world's most popular board design, the three-fin thruster.*

Most surfers know Simon's story, but there are parts of his story that affect me and that few people know. This is an example of surfers at their best, and how a spirit of generosity can occur even between two rivals at the highest level of competition.

Let me preface Simon's story by saying that the amazing year he had in 1981—bringing out his thruster and winning three contests on tour (including the Pipeline Masters), and in the process revolutionizing modern surfboard design—all unfolded at the lowest point in my own career because my father passed away that same year. Raised near the great surf in Narrabeen, in New South Wales (on the southern coast of Australia), Simon was one of the bigger guys on tour.

« Across countries and cultures surfers are connected not by nationality or religion or politics or age or sex but by their experience riding waves. »

At 6'3" and over 200 pounds, we called him «THE GENTLE GIANT» because of his easy-going nature. Fellow Australian Mark Richards had brought out his twin fin a couple of years prior, and by 1980 Mark had won two world titles. But Simon had problems with the twin-fin design. The two fins make the board very unstable compared to a single fin, and so the twin fin has to be ridden very precisely in small waves; in medium-to-large surf, the board is prone to slide out on turns. I think the way he surfed, he simply overpowered the twin fin because of his great size.

Another design popular at the time was the Lazor Zap, shaped by Australian Geoff McCoy (also from the New South Wales region). The Lazor Zap had a narrow nose, a wide tail, and a single fin. Basically a tear-drop shape. Simon was keeping an eye out for designs that would give him the maneuverability of a twin fin, but the stability—what we also call the positivity—of a single. He ended up *synthesizing the best qualities of the twin and the Lazor Zap,* and he came up with *the thruster: three fins, with a wide tail and narrow nose.* The design allowed him to maneuver sharply in smaller waves yet maintain control in the larger surf. The third fin actually did provide an additional «THRUST» to the board through turns.

The first time I saw Simon with the thruster was during a contest at Bells Beach, in Australia. I had switched to twin fins by then and had placed third on the world tour in 1980 — my best finish since winning the title in 1977. Things were going very well for me and I had every reason to believe they would get even better as I mastered the complexities of the twin fin. It was the opening of a new season on tour, and I had my sights set on another world title.

Then my father suddenly passed away. A heart attack. I got the call from my mother while I was in Australia, and for the first time in my life, I completely lost all motivation to surf. Not just to compete, but even to paddle out. We had been super close, obviously. He had been the number one motivating force in my life: my coach since I was a kid, my biggest fan, my inspiration. He had been present for every heat along the way, from my first victory in South Africa to my world title. Even afterward he continued to advise me on surfing equipment, my career, everything. I had been keen to surf for as long

« I had been keen to surf for as long as I could remember, but after my father passed away I hardly even wanted to look at a wave. It was a tough time. »

as I could remember, but after he passed away I hardly even wanted to look at a wave. It was a tough time.

Yet when I saw Simon's thruster, a little red flag raised up in the back of my mind. I was mindful about what had happened to me when Mark Richards brought out the twin fin — how it had taken me a year to recognize its benefits and to change over — and I did not want to get caught in a situation where I was *fighting another current, another riptide.* If there was a new trend starting up, I wanted to be ready to jump right in.

I had so many conflicting emotions at the time, moments of deep sadness for the loss of my father, yet I knew he would have advised me to keep competing; days would go by where I had no desire to go to the beach, and yet at the same time I was intrigued by the possibilities of Simon's board and the chance perhaps to redeem myself for past errors. There were actually days when I woke up and wanted to go surfing and to win, and then felt bad about my enthusiasm, as if somehow it were disrespectful to the memory of my father.

When I had first seen Simon on the beach with his board, I said to myself, Well, this design looks like it has merit. And our brief conversation went something like this:

«IS IT A GOOD BOARD THEN?»

«THREE WEEKS, MATE,» Simon said. «THREE WEEKS, AND YOU'LL BE RIDING ONE.» He laughed, because that is how confident he was.

«WELL,» I said, «YOU'RE MOST PROBABLY RIGHT.»

I had said it half-jokingly because Simon has a great sense of humor. He had not yet won any contests on the board, so I was interested but obviously not convinced.

Well, the surf came up every day during the contest, powerful waves that really played into Simon's strengths and the versatility of the thruster. While certainly not the most perfect wave in Australia, Bells Beach has perhaps the greatest tradition of surf competition in the country. Simon got a big boost for himself and his new design when he won the event. It was the first validation that his invention could not only hold its own against the best surfers in the world, but actually dominate the field. Most of us thought after the contest that Simon had indeed gotten himself a unique design.

But it was only one contest, and I was not quite ready to jump onto Simon's board. Like most professional athletes, surfers can be conservative when it comes to equipment. We spend countless hours in the waves trying different designs and refining what works for us, so we are not terribly inclined to abandon all that time and effort for something brand new. *Just because the thruster had worked for Simon at Bells Beach did not necessarily mean that it would work for someone else at another break.* No matter the sport, professional athletes will tell you that a great deal of success rides on having confidence in their equipment at critical moments. A surfer's quiver of boards might be likened to a golfer's bag of clubs—unless we are having serious problems, we generally stick with what we know and what has worked for us in the past.

Simon won the next event. The 2SM Coke Surfabout, which at the time was the richest surf contest in the world. Now that was two in a row. I had come up against Simon in the finals. As I say, I had switched over to twin fins and had beaten Mark Richards in the semifinals. We were surfing Simon's home break in Australia — north Narrabeen — and Simon smoked me. He was the only surfer in the world riding a three-fin thruster, and now after the first two contests he was ranked number one on the tour.

I did not need to wait any longer. After the final I phoned up Simon and told him very directly, «SIMON, I'D LOVE TO GET ONE OF THOSE BOARDS.»

Now here you have a situation where a guy is the top-ranked surfer in the world. He has come out with a fantastic new design that won him two contests right off the bat. He could have simply said no and hung up on me. I was one of Simon's biggest rivals. At the time I was rated number three or four in the world. We would compete against each other for the title the rest of the year: in South Africa, in Japan, in California, in France, and in the final events in the Hawaiian Islands.

Simon knew I was going through a rough period after my dad died. Still he could have let me down easy by saying, «I'M SORRY, SHAUN. I'M KEEPING THIS FOR MYSELF.» I would not have thought any less of him, and he certainly would have been completely within his rights.

You know what he told me? «OKAY.» He shaped me two thrusters just like that, and he gave them to me. Simon comes from a long tradition of great surfers who are also terrific shapers — Mark Richards is another example — and so it was the shaper in Simon who basically thought: «THIS IS A NEW DESIGN. IT'S WORKING GREAT FOR ME, AND I'VE WON TWO CONTESTS IN A ROW. OTHER SURFERS NEED TO RIDE THIS BOARD.»

« The natural world establishes a physical bond between all surfers through the bands of energy we ride. I try to strengthen this bond by focusing on common experiences and the things all surfers share. »

I was the first top pro surfer, other than Simon himself, to ride a three-fin thruster. He went on to win the final contest at Pipeline, but he did not capture the world title that year. He ended up ranked sixth in the world. It was a shame because he sprained his ankle during the contest in South Africa at Jeffreys Bay. It really was unfortunate because Simon had such a profound effect on surfboard design and has been responsible for increasing the enjoyment of so many people in waves around the world. Simon continues to live, surf, and shape in Australia, and top surfers like seven-time world champion Kelly Slater are still winning contests on his boards. Simon never patented his thruster design, *forsaking undoubtedly millions of dollars in revenue.* So the next time you see three fins on a board, think of Simon's three wins in 1981 and his incredible spirit of generosity.

Even when a surfer paddles out into the ocean and finds himself or herself alone in the lineup (which is getting harder to do these days), they understand that they form part of a larger community. Their actions do affect other people. When I paddle out at my local break I acknowledge this community by paddling around the impact zone and watching out for other surfers or by passing a wave along to someone else and passing along my knowledge to a young surfer who may need guidance. There are many forces that create divisions in surfing: localism, crowds, personal bias about the boards we ride and our styles of riding. Sometimes it seems a very human reaction when confronted with a new situation to categorize people by how they are different from us than by how we might share common goals. By any standard it is ridiculous to immediately dislike someone because he rides a longboard or because she chooses to ride waves on a board with three fins instead of one. *Yet it happens every day.*

I grew up in a divided society, and the positive things that came out of South Africa did so in spite of divisions, not because of them. The natural world establishes a physical bond between all surfers through the bands of energy we ride. I try to strengthen this bond by focusing on common experiences and the things all surfers share. I admit that it is harder to do; it also takes more patience and effort, but it is an effort we can take pride in. If surfers truly are different from other people, as I have said we are, then that pride comes from knowing that *we are creating an example for others to follow.* I always remind myself to stay ahead of the curve on this one, not behind it.

I Will Honor
the Sport of Kings

Duke Kahanamoku, father of modern surfing and at the time in 1965, the living embodiment of the aloha spirit (photo: Ron Stoner).

There is nothing more honorable than making a living by doing something you love. I have always felt a tremendous amount of pride calling myself a surfer. When I speak to groups of young people about *Surfer's Code,* I like to conclude with a bit of personal history about surfing and how that relates to their own experience in the water. «DON'T EVER ALLOW ANYONE TO BELITTLE WHAT YOU LOVE,» I tell them. «IF YOU'RE A SURFER, RESPECT THE SPORT, TREAT IT WITH HONOR, AND TAKE PRIDE IN WHAT YOU DO.» This will have more of a positive impact on the image of surfing than any amount of professional contests.

But my own pride in surfing, and my way of honoring the sport, did originate with surf contests. We were twenty-five or thirty men and women who formed the International Professional Surfers back in the mid-'70s, the first organization in surfing to hold a circuit of events around the world, and to crown a champion at the end. Competition had been a part of ancient Hawaiian surfing, and we knew these traditions and wanted to extend them around the world. With surf promoters Fred Hemmings and Randy Rarick leading the charge, we surfed fourteen events in five countries in 1976 and began realizing our dream of making a living out of a lifestyle. We thought surfing the most brave, honorable sport in the world, and we were going to tell everyone about it. Surfing had royal blood running through its veins, and we wanted to draw some of that blood for inspiration and be the modern *kings and queens of the waves.*

« We thought surfing the most brave, honorable

sport in the world. . . . Surfing had royal blood

running through its veins, and we wanted to

draw some of that blood for inspiration and be

the modern kings and queens of the waves. »

Most people at the time wondered how the words *professional*
and *surfer* could go together. I know that for many years surfing
was maligned in the United States. A strong anti-commercial senti-
ment ran through society during this period, fall-out from the coun-
terculture of the late 1960s. Making money was considered a sin in
many quarters, and commercialism (including contests) could only
corrupt a pure activity like surfing. At least this opinion was held by
the majority of surf magazine editors, the most influential of which
were all located in the States.

Surfing has a very different history in South Africa. With the
debut of the Gunston 500 in 1969 (first named the Durban 500 by
my father and the other founders), surfing took on a professional air
and surfers themselves were treated like golfers or ball players. The
sport never acquired the associations with drugs, drop-outs, or beach
bums that took hold in the States in the 1960s and '70s because of

popular Hollywood films. From a young age I approached surfing with
the belief that it was professional sport, and I have always felt an
obligation to counteract the negative image surfing has had in my
adopted country.

In those early years *we wanted to showcase surfing
as an incredible, exciting sport.* We wanted everyone to
know that surfers were every bit as professional as Joe Namath or
Jack Nicklaus. If we made a mistake during competition, more was at
stake than a sprained ankle or a pulled muscle. We put our lives on
the line at Pipeline and Waimea Bay, and people just had to recognize
our dedication as athletes. We were all convinced pro surfing would
happen, and that it would be our way to honor the sport.

We had a lot of naïveté back then, mixed in with our great love
and enthusiasm for surfing. We did not explode onto the world stage
as I thought we would, but we were a dedicated troupe of performers.
After I won the world title in 1977 I truly believed that it would be a
springboard to broader career opportunities. I hired an agent and
tried to promote myself as much as possible, but all my efforts simply
fizzled. I became depressed about the whole situation, actually. What
better opportunity would I ever have to gain mainstream recognition
for myself and for the sport than as World Champion?

I did succeed more in later years, but *recognition came
slowly* — success with Instinct and sponsorship from O'Neill; a
Calvin Klein ad here, a movie role there. With the growth of surfing
and the increasing popularity and clout of the surf industry, surfers
are now gaining many more opportunities to broaden their career
paths, and every pro surfer has that original group of men and women

to thank for their passion and dedication. A seminal moment occurred for the history of surfing way back in 1908, the founding of the Outrigger Canoe Club at Waikiki—the first official organization to promote surfing. A great resurgence of interest followed, and the sport has hardly slowed since. The first group of professional surfers formed a new Outrigger Club in a way: we organized and promoted the sport, and much of the incredible interest in surfing in the world today can be directly traced to that group effort.

Sometimes at one of those gatherings where I speak, a young person will ask, «WHAT MAKES SURFING SO SPECIAL?» Although I usually know that question is coming, I never have a simple answer. The experience of surfing, like any strong feeling, is hard to organize into words. There is a certain amount of faith involved, I end up saying; that leap into the unknown that makes every new step in life worth taking. *Part of the appeal of surfing is that you never really know what you are going to get.* I walk down the beach. I have my board and my wax and certain hopes, but I never really know what is in store for me. I might ride five of the best waves of my life in half an hour. Or I might sit there for three hours and catch nothing. Normally we want to remove uncertainty from our lives, but *surfing is all about uncertainty.* That feeling of taking a risk, that leap of faith every time I jump into the ocean, that paddle out among things unseen—all of these make surfing very special.

Or I might give them an answer by way of a story. There is a storm far out at sea sending invisible bands of energy my way. I stand on the beach and see that energy arrive in the form of ocean waves, much as *aumakua*—guardian gods in Hawaiian culture—can appear in the form of sharks to interact with humans. But that is not their true form. When I catch one of those bands of energy, stand on top of the wave and look down, I see the world from a unique perspective. I feel connected to the world in a special way. As a young boy riding waves in the Bay of Plenty in South Africa, I sat immersed in the water as that big red orb rose up over the horizon. I reveled in the sensation of floating, the feeling of being a part of a natural world where there were no divisions such as those existing on land. These moments provided an escape for me even then, and *a private act of defiance against a system that thrived on fear and control.*

I have referred to surfing as a sport in these lessons, mostly for convenience. There is no one word that expresses its full range of meanings, at least in English. *He'e nalu*—the Hawaiian term for surfing—undoubtedly captures the nuances more completely. Surfing is a sport for those who compete, and certainly this has been a big part of my life. But surfing has always meant more to me. When I sit at my desk and desperately need a break from phone calls and spreadsheets, I never replay in my mind winning a contest. Ultimately, I suppose, *I did not surf to compete; I competed so that I could surf.*

Outside of competition, surfing has no structure. There is no body of rules and regulations, and perhaps this is why surfers have developed their own codes. There is no ball to hit down a fairway. Surfing is all rough—everything is out of bounds. We have no lanes, no lines, no nylon nets to limit our expression. We are not aiming for par and are not aiming to beat someone.

Sign-up sheets? Reservations? No way. Come when you want, leave when you have taken your fill.

I always enjoy the questions of young people. They are so honest and usually get right to the heart of the matter. I have found different ways to answer them. But as I grow older, I have had less success answering similar questions for myself: *Where is surfing in my life?* For many years now surfing has been purely driven by sensation. My exhilaration, my validation has not come from beating an opponent or having a particular ranking at the end of the day. In some ways I felt that I had traveled back to the beginning. All the years I spent as a professional traveling the world, interacting with so many different cultures, helped me to understand the experiences I had riding waves as a child, in those days of riding waves for pure sensation.

Yet on a recent trip back to South Africa—I was invited to do color commentary on a world tour event at Jeffreys Bay—those same questions I thought I had answered resurfaced. I had recently turned fifty. The changes that I remarked upon this time were not in the country itself but within me. The anticipation of surfing Jeffreys Bay again—I had not ridden the break in twelve years—with the top

« Surfing is a sport for those who compete, and certainly this has been a big part of my life. But surfing has always meant more to me. »

professionals in the world pulled me back into a competitive mode. *How would I perform with the likes of Kelly Slater, Andy Irons, and Mick Fanning?* Not that I would be competing directly against them, of course, but would I even be able to hold my own in the water?

These issues resonated even more strongly because I was returning to a wave that had essentially defined my career. Jeffreys Bay — or J-Bay as surfers call it — is a beautiful, right-handed point break that sits at the bottom of South Africa up from the Cape of Good Hope, about six hundred miles down the coast from my hometown of Durban. Receiving the brunt of ferocious Antarctic storms, J-Bay can produce fantastic waves that — on those rare days when all five points line up — peel for a thousand yards and more. That is twice the length of Rincon, which is among the longest waves in California. **J-Bay is certainly among the top ten breaks in the entire world,** *if not the top five.* Beyond being a massively long wave, J-Bay peels enormously fast, perfect for my style of surfing. My signature moves — power carving and tube riding — had in large part been refined on the long walls and freight-train tubes of the break, and my reputation in the 1970s and '80s became irrevocably linked to this surfing spot.

So I had experience on my side and a wave that suited me well, all of which was comforting. Also, J-Bay is a truly experienced surfer's wave. What I mean by that is the break remains among the most technically challenging in the world. Surfers must have a different philosophy when they ride the place because **the wave will highlight their greatest skills as well as their most obvious weaknesses:** any skate-ramp maneuvers or flashy aerials will immediately leave them on the sidelines watching the wave steamroll past. You do not need to be extremely fit to surf the place, or to have buckets of courage required by such spots as Pipeline or Waimea Bay. You simply need to have an understanding of how energy works, and how to connect one fluid line with another over a very broad and moving canvas. Imagine a wave that requires the speed and grace of an ice skater along with the focus and balance of a tightrope walker. *If you do not possess such skills, the wave will blow by you faster than a runaway train.* The canvas of wave at J-Bay is so broad, yet that perfect line that takes you from one end to the other is no wider than a rope stretched between two buildings. *Only a few surfers can find that line and draw it out,* control the ride so that it becomes an inspired artistic performance rather than simply a body crossing from one end to the other. I understood all of this intimately, and yet it had been so long since I had surfed J-Bay that I did not know if, by day's end, I would play the part of the artist or the amateur.

So I stood on the beach before my first session and felt quite nervous. I tried not to show it. I greeted old friends — perhaps a little too enthusiastically — as I waxed up my board. I conversed with some of the pros on tour before paddling out, a couple of whom were half my age. Their manner was relaxed, exuding the confidence that surfing the best spots in the world on a regular basis will give you. They were in peak condition, of course, their skills honed finer even than the delicate boards they rode. I remembered that feeling of confidence. Outside I projected an air of casual excitement; inside my stomach roared along with the new swell that had marched into Jeffreys that morning. It was July—a winter month in South Africa—and I had been working on this book, so all the lessons I had learned through-out my surfing life were fresh in my mind. But even more present as I jumped into the ocean and began to stroke out to the lineup was an extremely powerful sense of place. All the memories of past sessions came rushing back to me, triggered by the physical act of paddling through the water. That sensation, and the emotions surrounding it, suddenly gave me an enormous boost of confidence. I felt that I could hold my own in the water.

> *I did not realize that, even at fifty, I still had lessons to learn from the ocean.*

As the first hour settled into the second, and the second into the third, my body fell into a rhythm I had not expected. I was surfing with the top competitors in the world, and yet I did not feel the need or desire to compete with them; rather their high level of performance inspired me to focus my attention internally. After several waves I had found that line of energy on the wave as precisely as a needle drops into the groove on a record. The music I heard from beginning to end became a profound sense of satisfaction as the waves rolled in and the third hour turned into the fourth and the fifth and the sixth.

In the seventh hour of my session at J-Bay I rode a wave that I could not have ridden better at the age of twenty. How do I know? Because after I kicked out of that wave, at the limits of exhaustion, I felt an exhilaration that I had felt back when I was the top competitor in the world. That was my standard. Not points on a scoreboard or my ranking at the end of the day, but the raw passion that comes from doing something you love and feeling as if you could not possibly have given any more of yourself. I felt so fortunate, as a surfer, to have the opportunity to express that passion on such a dynamic medium. So often in life we fall into the habit of allowing others to define our accomplishments, or to set the perimeters for our satisfaction. After I finished riding that last wave, I did not need anyone to paddle up and tell me what a great ride it was or to have it written up in a magazine. *In the end my personal sense of satisfaction was enough.*

It only took me seven hours to learn that lesson.

Surfing is one of the most ancient sports in the world. Practiced by Polynesians for countless centuries before Westerners first witnessed it in the eighteenth century, surfing survived when many other native activities did not. Disease, depopulation, religion, whaling ships, the California gold rush, Western customs — all contributed over two centuries to the decline of surfing.

Surfing survived. Against all probability and adversity, it survived. This is perhaps the best testament to why it is special. Surfing not only survived, but has now prospered to touch the lives of millions around the world every day. We honor surfing simply by paddling out and keeping the culture of riding waves alive. *We honor surfing by telling stories—by reading the stories of our shared traditions and passing them along to others.*

I know the most important reason why surfing survived. It is great fun. So go catch a wave, and tell someone about it.

My North Shore quiver of single-fin round pintail surfboards—from 7'0" to 9'0" and equipped to take on anything from small waves at Off The Wall to giant surf at Waimea Bay, December 1975 (photo: Jeff Divine).

Epilogue

As this book was going to press I received the terrible news from my wife that our only child, Mathew, had died while attending school in South Africa. The thoughts contained in this book were developed with him in the forefront of my mind at all times and are meant to be passed on from a parent to a child. I didn't want to stop publication of this book, as I wanted the *Surfer's Code* to always be a tribute to my wonderful young son whose soul will always burn brightly in everyone who knew him.

One week after his death, my wife and I sent this letter out to the world's surfing community, and I would like to share it with you:

Our beautiful fifteen-year-old son, Mathew Tomson, lost his life in a tragic schoolboy accident on Monday evening, April 24, 2006, in Durban, South Africa. Other than telling me how excited he was to play in his first rugby match the next day and that he loved me, the words in the following story were the last he spoke to me on the phone, across the oceans from South Africa to Santa Barbara. He had recently been enrolled at my old school, Clifton, one of South Africa's finest educational establishments and was loving its rigorous challenges. My remarkable wife was enjoying devoting all her efforts to Mathew and to just being a mom. He was making excellent academic progress and his easy smile, warm personality, mischievous sense of humor, and good looks had surrounded him with a circle of wonderful new friends. He was effervescent and laughing and looking forward to seeing me in the next few weeks.

An hour after the phone call he was dead, from a prank gone awry. Our boy loved life and life loved him back. He liked surfing, but it wasn't an obsession in his life. He loved his downhill bike and liked going fast and riding radically. It took skill and balance, something he innately possessed. He liked swimming and water polo, and we had some great days together body surfing and getting bombed in the wild shore break at Waimea Bay in Hawai'i.

He was truly thriving in his new school, and each time I spoke to him over the phone I could hear the wonderful happiness resonating through his voice. On that Monday, an hour before he died, he was so proud to read me what he'd written and read in English class that day, and my wife and I would like to share his beautiful words with our surfing friends all over the world. As a young boy he knew instinctively why we surfers love what we do and had the sensitivity to understand the subtle interplay between aloha and respect.

My wife Carla and I will miss him more than the depth of the oceans and the breadth of the sky. Hold your children tight and then hold them tighter again. Love them with everything you have, every minute of every second of every day. Teach them the right way and from us, teach them that they are not invincible.

With our love and with our deep sadness,
Shaun and Carla Tomson

Becoming a Man

Deep inside the barrel, completely in tune with my inner self, nothing else matters, the hard wind and spit shooting past me from behind, my hand dragging along the wall, the light shines ahead. My long hair carried by the wind. My feet are in perfect placement on the board. As I lean forward I feel myself speeding up, getting faster and faster as the barrel starts to close. I crouch down until my legs burn, and then I pull out to the whole line-up cheering. My body tingles with joy and happiness. I finally felt respected.

I got back on my board and paddled to the outside. I turned my head to the right to find Keone and his crew paddling towards me. My joyful feeling disappeared as fast as they came. My mouth went dry and I was truly afraid. He stopped in front of me and raised his hand. I ducked, but no pain was to come. I opened my eyes and put my hand out and firmly grasped his hand. This was not a hand shake, it was a sign of respect. I looked into his eyes, and we paddled to the point together without saying a word. The moment was much more powerful than any words could explain. For the rest of the day I was allowed to take off on as many waves as I wanted. I could have never imagined being part of "The Crew" but I was and I will always be. That was the day I became a man.

by Mathew Tomson

Acknowledgements

Thanks to Glenn Hening, Jericho Poppler, and Matt Meyerson for organizing a conference that provided an opportunity for the authors to meet and from which this book developed. To Mike Moser for his help on the initial proposal, and Matt Warshaw for providing background material (and sharing his agent). To Alison Deming for her perceptive insights on early drafts, and Bob Houston and Jane Miller for offering inspiring seminars at the University of Arizona during the writing of this book. Thanks also to the photographers and filmmakers whose fine work enhances these lessons: James Cassimus, Bill Delaney, Jeff Divine, Glenn Dubock, Don King, Dan Merkel, Jeff Novak, Joli, Larry Pierce, Ron Stoner, Bruce Weber, and Steve Wilkings. We also wish to express sincere gratitude to our agent, Wendy Burton Brouws, for her patience and perseverance. Finally, thanks to our editor, Jennifer Maughan, and the rest of the creative team at Gibbs Smith.

Author Biographies

Shaun Tomson was 1977 World Champion on the International Professional Surfing tour. A native of South Africa, he spent fourteen years on the World Tour (1976–1989), nine of those years rated in the top six and 12 contest wins including a record-setting six-year winning streak (1972–77) in the Gunston 500 in South Africa. He has been featured in more than 40 surf videos, was profiled in an Outdoor Life Network documentary series (1998), and starred as a surf journalist in Tristar's picture *In God's Hands*.

Additional honors include nine appearances on the cover of *Surfer* and *Surfing* and an inductee on the Huntington Beach Surfing Walk of Fame (1997). He was most recently listed as one of the 25 most influential surfers of the century (*Surfer,* 1999) and one of the 16 greatest surfers of all time (*Surfing,* 2004). He is currently Chairman of the Advisory Board for The Surfrider Foundation and, with his wife, Carla, directs the apparel company, Solitude, in Santa Barbara, California.

Patrick Moser is Chair of the Department of Languages at Drury University where he teaches a course on the history and culture of surfing. He has written articles for *Surfer, Surf Life for Women,* and *The Surfer's Journal*. He is currently completing an anthology of surf writings entitled *He'e Nalu: Changing Images of Surfriding* and also working on his first novel in the writing program at the University of Arizona.

Photo Credits

James Cassimus: front cover photo
Bill Delaney: pages 66–67
Jeff Divine: pages 46–47, 186–187
Glenn Dubock: pages 106–107
Don King: pages 60–61
Dan Merkel: pages 19, 26–27, 78–79, 120, 170–171

Jeff Novak: pages 138–139
Joli: pages 146–147
Larry Pierce: pages 94–95
Ron Stoner: pages 41, 174
Bruce Weber: page 138
Steve Wilkings: pages 34–35, 132–133